How to Win at Spread Betting

**An analysis of why some people win,
some lose and how you can be a winner**

By Alpesh B. Patel & Paresh H. Kiri

 Harriman House

HARRIMAN HOUSE LTD

3A Penns Road
Petersfield
Hampshire
GU32 2EW
GREAT BRITAIN

Tel: +44 (0)1730 233870
Email: enquiries@harriman-house.com
Website: www.harriman-house.com

First published in Great Britain in 2013

Copyright © Harriman House Ltd

The right of Alpesh B. Patel and Paresh H. Kiri to be identified as Authors has been asserted in accordance with the Copyright, Design and Patents Act 1988.

ISBN: 978-0-85719-341-4

British Library Cataloguing in Publication Data
A CIP catalogue record for this book can be obtained from the British Library.

Contents

eBook edition

As a buyer of the print edition of *How to Win at Spread Betting* you can now download the eBook edition free of charge to read on an eBook reader, your smartphone or your computer. Go to:

ebooks.harriman-house.com/winSBebook

or point your smartphone at the QRC below.

You can then register and download your free eBook.

Follow us, like us and watch us...

@HarrimanHouse
www.linkedin.com/company/harriman-house
www.facebook.com/harrimanhouse
www.youtube.com/harrimanhouse

www.harriman-house.com

About the Authors

Alpesh B. Patel

Alpesh is co-founder of asset manager Praefinium Partners and **www.alpeshpatel.com** and has had over 200 columns on trading published by the *Financial Times* in his 'The Diary of an Internet Trader' column. Alpesh is a former Visiting Fellow in Business at Corpus Christi College, Oxford University and a qualified barrister. He won the competition in the *Financial Times* to predict the value of the FTSE 100 over a 12 month period, coming within 0.5% of the final value. For Bloomberg TV he presented trading shows for three years.

Alpesh has lectured on trading in Beijing, Hong Kong, Singapore, Guatemala, Spain, Dubai and San Francisco and his trading books have been translated into German, French, Russian, Thai, Korean and Polish. Alpesh's trading blog is available at **www.alpeshpatel.com/blog**.

Past clients of Alpesh's company for customer acquisition include Barclays, Goldman Sachs, American Express, Merrill Lynch, HSBC and all the major spread betting companies.

Paresh H. Kiri

Paresh has vast experience as a floor trader on the world's second largest derivatives exchange, LIFFE, and as a portfolio manager for 18 years. He is an FSA regulated Investment Manager.

Starting his career on the LIFFE floor in 1993, Paresh was one of the first traders to embrace screen trading, through the LIFFE online trading platform APT – Automated Pit Trading. Making progress under the guidance of the legendary LIFFE trader David Kyte, he was one of the most consistent traders on the largest product on the floor – the Japanese Government Bond.

After successfully completing the Investment Management Certificate in 1996 he was one of the founders of Kyte Securities. From trading financial futures and option products, Paresh had his first taste of trading shares. During the next three years he was instrumental in discovering bespoke strategies for trading equities globally.

In 2000, Kyte Securities became Eden Financial – which is now one of the most respected wealth management companies in the City of London, and the strategies developed were then incorporated as the backbone to the Tomahawk hedge fund, run by Marble Bar Asset Management.

Since leaving Eden Financial in 1999, Paresh has been managing private client and institutional money. He has also been developing an Index Options Desk, and seeking ways of bringing the strategies he developed to the wider public audience by structuring managed accounts services using online trading platforms.

Paresh regularly coaches and holds private seminars on trading the markets.

Alpesh dedication

For Aekta

United your resolve, United your hearts;
United be your mind, Thus you live long together.
(Rig Veda, 10-191-4)

Paresh dedication

For Rajee

Who took the biggest gamble on me, and is still waiting
for the bet to pay off

Introduction

We believe that no other book has ever provided the kind of essential hard information traders need to win in spread betting as we do in this book.

In writing this book we took data from the daily trades of hundreds of traders over a five-year period – tens of thousands of trades. Then we analysed it. This analysis allows us to reveal in this book:

- Which clients win and lose? What are their characteristics (age, experience, income, gender, location, etc)?

- Which markets are the easiest to make money on?

- Which markets should retail investors avoid?

- Do investors make more money in volatile markets or quiet markets?

- Which is more profitable: to go long or to go short?

- Do short-term/day traders make more money than long-term traders?

- What are the most common mistakes made by losing clients?

- How much do the top spread bettors actually make?

- Which trading systems work best?

- Do technical analyst traders following price charts outperform fundamental analysis traders?

- Do online traders make more money than telephone traders?

- How long are the most profitable positions held?

- What impact do dealing costs have on your ability to beat the market?

- What rules do profitable traders use for setting trade size and stop-losses?

- How did one trader who had not traded before get 450 winning trades out of 454?

- What do winners do differently from losing spread betting traders?

- What size accounts do the most profitable traders have?

- How many spread bettors win and how many lose?

- Do losers become winners and winners become losers over time?

- Do winners and losers skew bets when they are winning or losing?

- How long do winning traders hold on to losing bets? How long do losers hold on to winning and losing bets?

- Do winners add to losing bets or winning bets compared to how losers treat winning and losing positions?

- Do winners mimic what big winners like George Soros do?

What does success look like?

What puts someone in the top 10 of spread bettors?

Figure 0.1 shows the profits by some of the largest spread bettors from one company.

What are they doing right?

That is what this book teaches.

Figure 0.1: Spreadex winners

Source: Spreadex

For example, Figure 0.2 shows one of the most successful trading periods of one of the spread betting traders we analysed. The horizontal axis shows how much money was made in each trade. The vertical axis shows the numbers of trades. Notice he did 454 trades in a two week period – in other words this was no lucky fluke. All but four of those trades made money! Most surprising, two months earlier this person had never spread bet in their life!

Figure 0.2: A successful trading period

Individual Closed Trades Returns 1st – 17th July 2009

The Managed Account Commenced in June 2009 on five accounts. All accounts show returns between +30% to +100% on capital deposited

•Total trades: 454 trades (excl funding overnight funding charges)
•Winning trades: 450
•Losing trades: 4
•Average return: £14.79 (after all overnight funding charges costs)
•Maximum: £500. Minimum: £-35
•Total overnight funding charges: £408.75
•Image below: all trades, including overnight funding charges

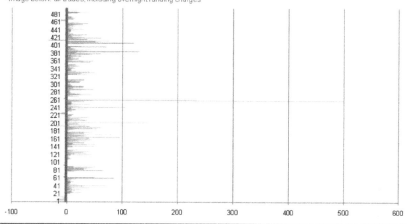

It is this type of hardcore insider data we will dissect.

What did they do?

What was their trading strategy?

All is revealed in this book.

Figure 0.3 is a graphical chart of the performance of the first fund Alpesh launched. We dissect data not just from other traders but also our own trading.

Figure 0.3: The performance of the first fund Alpesh launched

We have analysed thousands of trades to show you common characteristics of when winners win and lose and when losers win and lose, and what differentiates a winner from a loser.

By the way, we define a winner as someone who consistently makes profits from trading over a prolonged period of time – i.e. not a one-hit wonder.

We are introducing you to graphs like this because we will slice and dice them until you fully understand what differentiates winners from losers.

As insiders, our aim is to show you how to beat the market. We know it can be done, because we know the winners who do it. In this book, we show you how they do it.

Our favourite type of trading

For us, spread betting works best because it is suited to momentum or swing trading. It allows us to follow trends, whereas buy and hold may leave us with no returns after a long time. Spread bets also allow us to short (that is, to profit from falling markets as easily as rising ones).

Figure 0.4: Profits from rising and falling markets

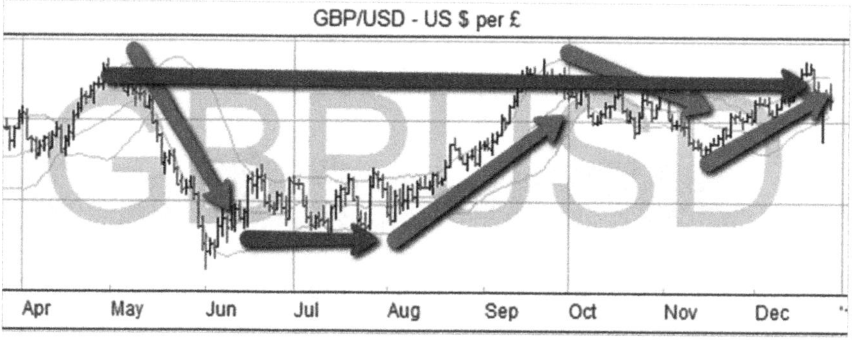

Created by us using Alpesh Patel Special Edition of Sharescope

By doing this type of trading we can take less risk – because we can jump in and out of the market and are not always exposed to it. And thanks to modern technology, we no longer need to be at a bank to get access to trading platforms for instant execution and news. What traders lack is know-how and it is our job to provide know-how.

But there are other reasons why such types of trading are so popular. Professional fund managers use momentum strategies and have become very profitable as a result. (NB. We use the terms momentum, swing and trend interchangeably throughout this book.)

Figure 0.5: A Momentum or Swing Trading or Trend Following Fund

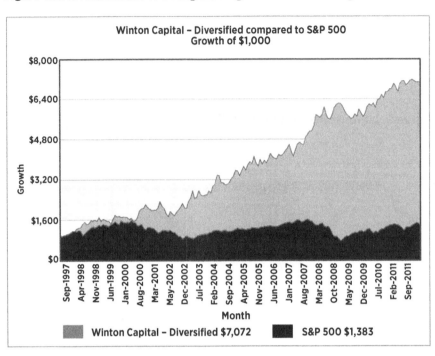

Source: Winton Capital

The best traders in the funds following such momentum strategies make hundreds of millions. For example:

- Bruce Kovner is worth more than $4.5 billion.
- John W. Henry is worth $840 million.
- Bill Dunn made $80 million in 2008.
- Michael Marcus turned an initial $30,000 into $80 million.
- David Harding is now worth more than $690 million.
- Ed Seykota turned $5,000 into $15 million over 12 years.
- Kenneth Tropin made $120 million in 2008.
- Larry Hite has made millions upon millions over 30 years.
- Louis Bacon is worth $1.5 billion.
- Paul Tudor Jones is worth $3.3 billion.
- Trend following trader Man Group trades $68.6 billion in assets.

Alpesh B. Patel
Paresh Kiri

Chapter 1

Winners Are Not Professionals – But You Need to be Professional to be a Winner

"Be willing to make decisions. That's the most important quality in a good leader. Don't fall victim to what I call the ready-aim-aim-aim syndrome. You must be willing to fire."

– T. Boone Pickens

The big answers

So when we analysed the data from the spread bettors, what did we find in relation to the big questions?

Which markets are the easiest to make money in?

Did spread bettors make money in niche markets – such as coffee futures – or in the more liquid popular markets, such as FTSE 100?

We found that the proportion of winners to losers and amounts won on average per trader did not vary markedly among the different markets. However, because relatively few traded lesser known markets, it would not be right to base conclusions upon this.

As for the more popular markets, such as Dow and FTSE, we could not say it was easier to make money on these from the proportion of winning traders' average and largest wins. Whilst there was the occasional outlier – large wins on lesser known small stocks or contracts – these could easily be due to superior niche knowledge or just statistically not something we can draw a strong conclusion from.

Our data for FX trades is shown later in the book; this shows marked differences of success depending on the FX pair. From a cause and effect perspective we assume that all traders in each market were of a variety of abilities, and not that the best traders congregated to certain markets.

The average profit per trader did rise when markets showed prolonged trends, as one would expect. For instance, in the case of gold in 2009 and 2010 and oil in 2008 and 2009. Of course, the problem is knowing which markets are about to start a prolonged trend!

We know spread betting firms do bet against private investors – they will take the other side of the bet and not hedge in the market because they know most clients lose money. They also will hedge 110%+ consistently winning traders. But of course the only way to know this information is to actually work inside a spread betting firm!

Which markets should retail investors avoid?

Winning traders tended to focus at any one time on around four markets. They traded these extensively and were intimately knowledgeable about them. When asked why they did not trade just one market, or dozens, the reason was that they wanted to find the right mix between having trading opportunities and market knowledge.

However, whilst you would expect winning traders to win across all those markets, what was surprising is that a winning trader could be a winner across three products, but consistently be a loser on a fourth.

We also found the following information very instructive based on analysis of 12 million FX trades:

Figure 1.1: Winning/losing trades for various currency pairs

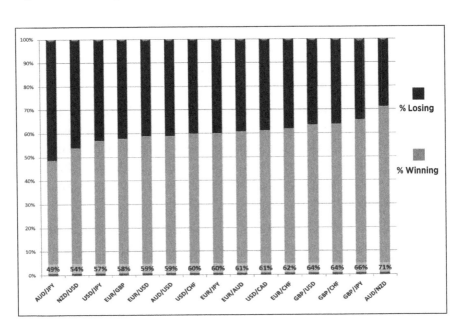

Source: © FXCM

Figure 1.2: Profit/loss for various currency pairs

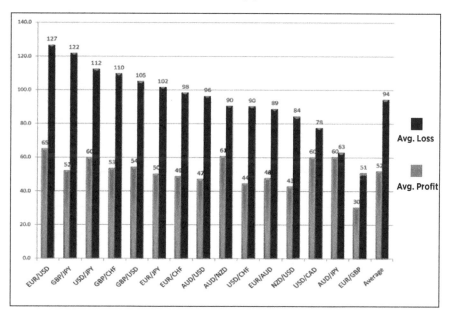

Do investors make more money in volatile markets or quiet markets?

Our research found traders made most money in markets which fell between volatile and quiet. This was because although more started trading during extreme volatile times, such as the credit crunch, that did not necessarily translate into profits.

Let's take a look at the average pip movement of the major currency pairs during each trading session.

Figure 1.3: Comparison of volatility levels for various currency pairs

Pair	Tokyo	London	New York
EUR/USD	76	**114**	92
GBP/USD	92	**127**	99
USD/JPY	51	**66**	59
AUD/USD	77	**83**	81
NZD/USD	62	**72**	70
USD/CAD	57	**96**	96
USD/CHF	67	**102**	83
EUR/JPY	102	**129**	107
GBP/JPY	98	**107**	103
EUR/GBP	78	**61**	47
EUR/CHF	79	**109**	84

Source: © FXCM

From the table you will see that the European session normally provides the most movement.

Figure 1.4: Comparison of profitability by time frame for 5 currency pairs

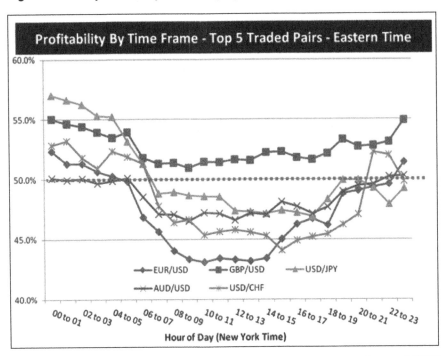

Source: © FXCM

Which is more profitable: to go long or to go short?

We found traders made money more quickly on their shorts than their longs; but overall the total profits from longs and shorts were about the same. So although markets generally fall quicker than they rise, the total profits from each side is about the same.

Do short-term/day traders make more money than long-term traders?

Although research shows market timing (i.e. short-term trading) is very difficult to get right, our target market tended to be almost all short-term traders. It would be rare for any to hold positions longer than 3-4 months. This may be because this type of trading attracts short-term traders or because funding charges lead to action being taken to exit trades. Also, the ease of online trading may encourage trading over longer term investment.

One other way we analysed this was to capture a certain number of points per week. We take the example of the FTSE 100. We assume a stop-loss of 2xATR (average true range) and a bet size of £10 per point.

Figure 1.5: Analysis of profitability by frequency of trading

Time frame	Number of signals per week	Typical price range in period pips	2 x ATR	Gbp10 per point stop-loss	Capital if stop- loss is 2%
1m	85	1.5	3	Gbp30	Gbp 1,500
5m	20	2.5	5	Gbp50	Gbp 2,500
30m	3	13	26	Gbp260	Gbp 13,000
1h	1.5	20	40	Gbp400	Gbp 20,000
4h	0.5	30	60	Gbp600	Gbp 30,000
1d	0.25	65	130	Gbp 1,300	Gbo 65,00

© Alpesh Patel

Time frame	Number of signals per weel	2 x ATR	Points captured on win per week*	Points lost on losses per week	New points gained per week
1m	85	3	765	510	255
5m	20	5	300	200	100
30m	3	26	234	156	78
1h	1.5	40	180	120	60
4h	0.5	60	90	60	30
1d	0.25	130	97.5	65	32.5

*Assume only correct 50% of the time. Assume capture 3xATR when correct and lose 2xATR when wrong

© **Alpesh Patel**

So on that basis we found that to hit the profitability goals targets could be met by trading shorter time frames (but these are more time-consuming of course), or increasing the trading capital size, or increasing the risk per trade to 3% of trading capital on a stop-loss – but again that means more risk. So there are tradeoffs but it has to be thought out systematically.

In theory one would expect more profits from trying to time the market. But it was very few who were consistently able to profit from short-term trading and get the timing right. In this book we show how. But we should be aware, as the Figure 1.6 shows, even the best hedge fund managers are not consistently successful:

Figure 1.6: Performance of hedge fund styles (2000-2012)

2000	2001	2002	2003	2004	2005	2006	2007	2008	2009	2010	2011	2012
							Emg Mkts 20.3%					
Conv Arb 25.6%			Emg Mkts 28.8%	Distr Secs 15.6%		Emg Mkts 20.5%	Global Macro 17.4%					
Short Bias 15.8%	Distr Secs 20.0%		Distr Secs 23.1%	Emg Mkts 12.5%	Emg Mkts 17.4%	Distr Secs 15.6%	L/S Equity 13.7%		Conv Arb 47.4%	Global Macro 13.5%		Distr Secs 11.6%
Eq Mkt Neutral 15.0%	Global Macro 18.4%	Mgd Futures 18.3%	Global Macro 18.0%	L/S Equity 11.6%	Short Bias 17.0%	Multi-Strat 14.5%	Multi-Strat 10.1%		Emg Mkts 30.0%	Fxd Inc Arb 12.5%		Multi-Strat 11.2%
Risk Arb 14.7%	Conv Arb 14.6%	Short Bias 18.1%	L/S Equity 17.3%	Global Macro 8.5%	Distr Secs 11.7%	L/S Equity 14.4%	Eq Mkt Neutral 9.3%		Fxd Inc Arb 27.4%	Mgd Futures 12.2%	Global Macro 6.4%	Fxd Inc Arb 11.0%
Global Macro 11.8%	Eq Mkt Neutral 9.3%	Global Macro 14.7%	Multi-Strat 15.0%	Multi-Strat 7.6%	L/S Equity 9.7%	Conv Arb 14.3%	Risk Arb 8.6%		Multi-Strat 24.6%	Emg Mkts 11.3%	Fxd Inc Arb 4.7%	Emg Mkts 10.3%
Multi-Strat 11.2%	Fxd Inc Arb 8.0%	Eq Mkt Neutral 7.4%	Mgd Futures 14.1%	Fxd Inc Arb 6.9%	Global Macro 9.2%	Global Macro 13.5%	Distr Secs 8.4%		Distr Secs 21.0%	Conv Arb 11.0%	Eq Mkt Neutral 4.5%	L/S Equity 8.2%
Fxd Inc Arb 6.3%	Emg Mkts 5.8%	Emg Mkts 7.4%	Conv Arb 12.9%	Eq Mkt Neutral 6.5%	Multi-Strat 7.5%	Eq Mkt Neutral 11.2%	Short Bias 6.0%		L/S Equity 19.5%	Distr Secs 10.3%	Short Bias 3.8%	Conv Arb 7.8%
Mgd Futures 4.2%	Risk Arb 5.7%	Multi-Strat 6.3%	Risk Arb 9.0%	Mgd Futures 6.0%	Eq Mkt Neutral 6.1%	Fxd Inc Arb 8.7%	Mgd Futures 6.0%		Risk Arb 12.0%	Multi-Strat 9.3%	Multi-Strat 1.3%	Global Macro 4.6%
L/S Equity 2.1%	Multi-Strat 5.5%	Fxd Inc Arb 5.8%	Fxd Inc Arb 8.0%	Risk Arb 5.5%	Risk Arb 3.1%	Risk Arb 8.1%	Conv Arb 5.2%	Mgd Futures 18.3%	Global Macro 11.6%	L/S Equity 9.3%	Conv Arb 1.1%	Risk Arb 2.8%
Distr Secs 1.9%	Mgd Futures 1.9%	Conv Arb 4.0%	Eq Mkt Neutral 7.1%	Conv Arb 2.0%	Fxd Inc Arb 0.6%	Mgd Futures 8.1%	Fxd Inc Arb 3.6%	Short Bias 14.9%	Eq Mkt Neutral 4.1%	Risk Arb 3.2%	Risk Arb 0.8%	Eq Mkt Neutral 0.8%
Emg Mkts -5.5%	Short Bias -3.6%	Distr Secs -0.7%	Short Bias -32.6%	Short Bias -7.7%	Mgd Futures -0.1%	Short Bias -6.6%		Risk Arb -3.3%	Mgd Futures -6.6%	Eq Mkt Neutral -0.9%	Mgd Futures -4.2%	Mgd Futures -2.9%
	L/S Equity -3.7%	L/S Equity +1.0%			Conv Arb -2.5%			Global Macro -4.6%	Short Bias -25.0%	Short Bias -22.5%	Distr Secs -4.2%	Short Bias -20.4%
		Risk Arb -3.5%						L/S Equity -19.8%			Emg Mkts -6.7%	
								Distr Secs -20.5%			L/S Equity -7.3%	
								Multi-Strat -23.6%				
								Fxd Inc Arb -28.8%				
								Emg Mkts -30.4%				
								Conv Arb -31.6%				

What all the winners had in common was that their losses were limited in size, not in number. That means whilst they may have had as many as 40% losing trades, the total size of those individual losses was controlled.

We found confirmation of this from both professional and retail winning traders. The following chart for instance shows a professional trader we first met in 1997. You can see this fund's ability in FX trading to cut the size of losses.

Figure 1.7: Distribution of monthly returns for Hathersage Asset Management

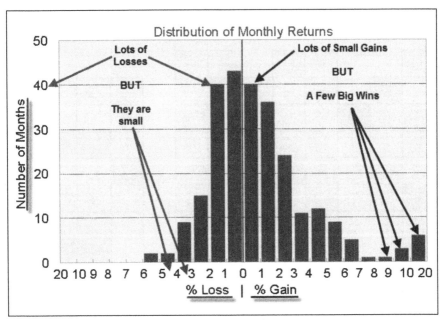

The above from Hathersage Asset Management run by Bill Lipschutz (who Alpesh interviewed) was a performance resulting from two characteristics that the best winning traders in spread betting firms had worked out:

1. that you bet small sizes, so on your losses you lose little, and

2. that you have a way of ensuring winning trades keep rising, and indeed add to winning positions at times, never to losing ones, and that you close losing trades quickly while losses are small.

An example of the effect such a strategy has on performance is shown in the following table where for FX trades a 40 pip stop-loss is applied.

Figure 1.8: 40 pip stop-loss

Date	Time	Buy or sell	Entry price	Date	Time	Buy or sell	Exit price	Profit or loss	Pips without stop-loss	Pips with 40 pip stop-loss
4/2/13	00:00:00	Sell	1.56979	8/2/13	04:00:00	Buy	1.57217	-0.00238	-24	-24
8/2/13	04:00:00	Buy	1.57187	12/2/13	04:00:00	Sell	1.56445	-0.00742	-74	-40
13/2/13	08:00:00	Sell	1.56475	19/2/13	08:00:00	Buy	1.54896	0.015795	158	158
Total Profit	60	94								

How did winners find their stop-loss levels?

The traders we spoke to would tend to look at their winning trades and place a stop-loss at levels which would not have led to being exited of those winning trades. Playing around with levels then allowed them to work out the correct level.

Amateur traders (a very few) also have professionalised their trading as the following figures show (for FX).

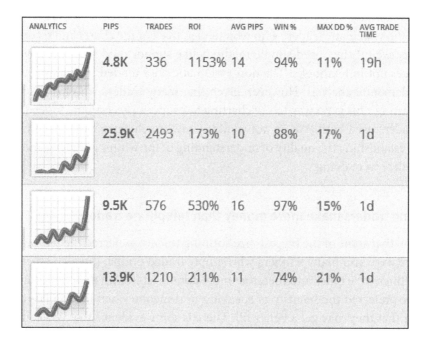

Again the characteristic of the winners was not just to keep the percentage of winning trades high, but more importantly their losses low (indirectly indicated by maximum drawdown number).

Which trading systems work best?

Winning traders were definitely systematic in their approach. They did not simply use a 'seat of pants' approach. They all used some method of timing – some way of finding momentum.

For FX traders this was usually either:

- *mean reversion*: where prices were expected to return to their recent average, or

- *breakout*: where prices were expected to continue in one direction outside and away from recent averages.

Popular techniques used were trendlines, MACD, Stochastics. But winning traders tended to use amended techniques in their strategies, they did not tend to use them in the same way as textbooks.

Do technical analyst traders following price charts outperform fundamental analysis traders?

Most of the systematic traders who won tended to examine charts and trade off those, even if they used simple methods like support and resistance, or techniques not in textbooks. The non-systematic ones tended to attempt to use fundamental analysis. However, given that many traders who lost also used charting, this is no way to say charting is a superior technique. Indeed, some traders used both. We do not want to draw conclusions based on this without establishing the quality of understanding of the winning traders, and of what they were doing.

Do online traders make more money than telephone traders?

We found that some of the biggest-size winning traders preferred the phone. But there were also many winners who simply traded online. It may be that the wealthier were older and therefore more comfortable with the phone, or that they preferred the security of speaking to someone when betting large sums, or that they may get a better fill. There is some evidence that you can get a better fill at some brokers if the broker on the phone is asked to work the order.

How long are the most profitable positions held?

As the table below shows there is a trade-off between the number of trading signals and the time taken to monitor. What we did find is that losing traders tended to hold their positions longer in their losing trades than their winning ones. Whereas winning traders tended to hold their winners for a longer duration than their losing positions. This verified our belief that winners had a way of letting winners run, and losing traders cut their winners short and let their losers run.

Also, an important correlation among losers was their tendency to add to losing positions. We found winners tended to add to winning positions.

Figure 1.9: Analysis of trading signals

Time frame	Number of signals per week	2 x ATR	Points captured on win per week*	Points lost on losses per week	Net points gained per week
1m	85	3	765	510	255
5m	20	5	300	200	100
30m	3	26	234	156	78
1h	1.5	40	180	120	60
4h	0.5	60	90	60	30
1d	0.25	130	97.5	65	32.5

© Alpesh Patel

What impact do dealing costs have on your ability to beat the market?

Successful traders understood the advantages of trading the most liquid markets – that the spreads were lower and that meant it was easier to beat the market. But despite this, our studies showed that even when brokers offered zero spreads trading, it was not simply a case of placing two mutually opposite trades with stop-losses at say 10 points and profit targets at 20 points – in the hope that even by random chance you would win overall.

We found that even on zero spread trading the chances of hitting, say, a 10 point stop was the same as hitting a 10 point profit – all things being equal. And the chances of hitting, say, a 12 point profit with a 10 point stop did not change that much so that in our sample trades it still meant just breaking even.

So you needed more than just random buy and sell signals and hoping your profit target being greater than your stop-loss would overall mean being profitable. You needed to trade with a momentum-based strategy to increase the odds of hitting that 12 profit target and reducing the odds of a 10 stop-loss being hit.

What size accounts do the most profitable traders have?

Whilst there is clearly a bare minimum account size below which trading is uneconomical, it was hard to discern a correlation between winning traders and account sizes. We simply could not say that winning traders had more money in their account.

However, we noted the flexibility that a larger account size offered winning traders in that they could afford to risk less of their capital per trade and therefore losing trades had less of an impact. If we consider for instance traders using a fixed stop-loss of 2 x ATR then winners tended to easily keep this to 2% of their trading capital. Also, if they had large account sizes then it made the profits in absolute terms big anyway.

We noted that the most successful traders understood the link between position sizing (bet size) and stop-loss and the impact on their account. They would for instance increase their stop-loss distance but reduce their position size so that they would lose less frequently but still only lose 2% of their trading capital for instance when they did.

An example will help understand this.

Figure 1.10: Analysis of size of account and stop-loss

ATR = 25 pips
2 x ATR = 50 pips
3 x ATR = 75 pips
Assume Total Risk Capital = 100k
2% of 100k = 2k = 2xATR (50 pips) = 40gbp per pip
2% of 100k = 2k = 3xATR (75 pips) = 27gbp per pip

2ATR

3ATR

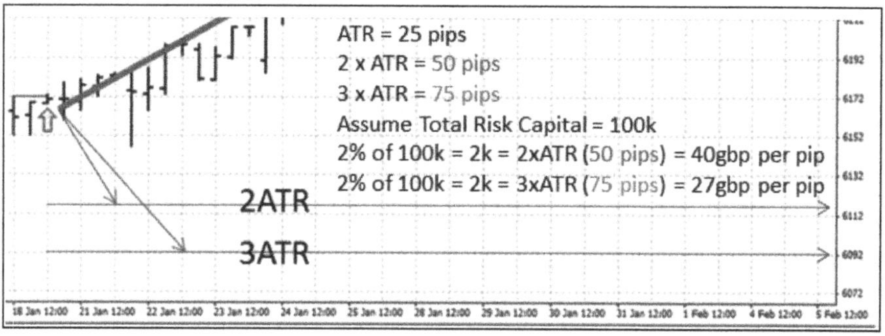

Created by Alpesh Patel using MT4 trading platform

Figure 1.11: Analysis of size of account and stop-loss

ATR	Benefit	Costs	Overall
2	Total loss is fixed – 2%	Stopped out more often of potentially profitable trades than if 2 x ATR	Win/loss ratio lower, but profitability higher on wins
3	Total loss is fixed – 2%	Position size smaller than if 2 x ATR so makes less profits on profitable trades	Win/loss ratio higher, but profitability lower on wins

© Alpesh Patel

How many spread bettors win and how many lose?

Although the majority of spread bettors lost in our analysis, the winners all had certain things in common:

- they tended to let **winners run**, and added to winning positions, and
- they **risked small amounts** of their overall trading capital.

Do losers become winners and winners become losers over time?

We found many examples of new accounts being opened where people doubled their money in a week or two only to be losing later – often due to increased bet size and frequency.

Our study was not able to accurately monitor how many losing traders became winners over a longer period.

Do winners and losers skew bets when they are winning or losing?

Winners definitely ran profits by adding to winning positions. One method is shown below.

Figure 1.12: High and Low method

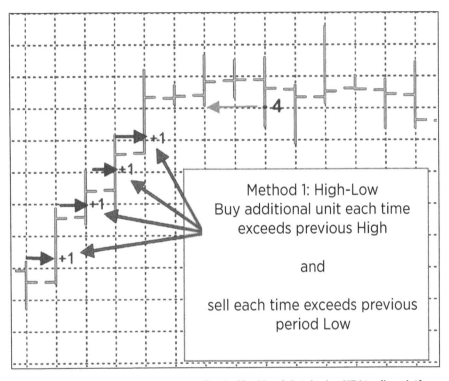

Created by Alpesh Patel using MT4 trading platform

Another method was the Average True Range Method (shown opposite).

Figure 1.13: Example

ATR = 1.20	
First position entered at	28.30
Second position entered at	28.30 + (0.5 x 1.20) or 28.9-0
Third position entered at	28.90 + (0.5 x 1.20) or 29.50
Fourth position entered at	29.50 + (0. 5x 1.20) or 30.10

If you do add additional positions then raise the initial 2 x ATR stop-loss to be 2 x ATR from latest entered position

ATR = 1.20	Entry price	Stop
First	28.30	25.90 i.e. 28.30 - (2 x 1.20)
Second	28.90	26.50 i.e. 25.90 + 0.5 x 1.20
Third	29.50	27.10
Fourth	30.10	27.70

Do winners mimic owning what big winners like George Soros does?

Like Soros, winners actually had a lot of losing trades – some lost 60% of the time. Whereas we had losers who won over 60% of the time. The key difference was that when winners won they sometimes won big and always lost small, whereas losers sometimes lost big and always won small.

From our interviews we found no evidence of winners trying to copy big traders like George Soros, although those who overall lost did look for the ownership patterns of well known traders. We assume this must have been for timing reasons that they owned the stocks of winning fund managers but still lost money. (Examples of the recent holdings of George Soros and Warren Buffett are given in the following two figures.)

Figure 1.14: Top holdings of George Soros

Below are the top holdings for George Soros as of 31/12/2012 based on the 13F filing filed on 14/2/2013. Total value of the portfolio is £4.6 billion.

Sym	Company	Price	Chg%	Market ▼ Cap	Earning-Yield
AAPL	Apple	633.85	+0.86%	584.08B	5.59%
GOOG	Google	633.72	+1.09%	203.03B	4.75%
WFC	Wells Fargo	33.70	+2.37%	173.60B	8.57%
PFE	Pfizer	22.07	+0.39%	169.00B	5.78%
PEP	PepsoCo	65.29	+0.68%	101.39B	6.21%
DIS	The Walt Disney Company	41.60	+1.49%	73.64B	6.44%
KFT	Kraft Foods	37.02	-0.01%	65.41B	5.38%
AMGN	Amgen	66.92	+1.10%	58.02B	6.10%
BIDU	Baidu	146.91	+1.72%	39.06B	2.05%
LOW	Lowe's Companies	30.92	+1.93%	37.99B	4.71%
GM	General Motors Company	24.08	+1.56%	37.10B	19.32%
TXN	Texas Instruments	31.98	+0.92%	36.21B	5.93%
FCX	Freeport-McMoran Copper & Gold	36.65	+0.05%	34.72B	13.05%
DTV	DIRECTTV	49.12	+1.47%	34.16B	7.17%
BBD	Banco Bradesco	16.95	+1.99%	31.78B	10.47%
WAG	Walgreens	32.97	+2.36%	28.14B	9.10%
MHS	Medco Health Solutions	70.30	+0.00%	27.22B	5.15%
ESRX	Express Scripts Holding Company	56.48	+1.77%	26.94B	4.56%
TWC	Time Warner Cable	79.36	+2.04%	24.82B	6.39%
VIA B	Viacom	46.27	+0.06%	23.16B	6.42%
CME	CME Group	285.93	+1.36%	18.73B	9.62%
YHOO	Yahoo!	14.92	-0.47%	18.59B	5.47%
WMB	Williams Companies	30.93	+1.21%	18.01B	2.06%

Source: GuruFocus.com

Figure 1.15: Top holdings of Warren Buffett

Investments

Below we show our common stock investments that at yearend had a market value of more than $1 billion. (12/3/11)

Shares	Company	Percentage of company owned	Cost*	Market
				(in millions)
151,610,700	American Express Company	13.0	$ 1,287	$ 7,151
200,000,000	The Coca-Cola Company	8.8	1,299	13,994
29,100,937	ConocoPhillips	2.3	2,027	2,121
63,905,931	International Business Machines Corp	5.5	10,856	11,751
31,416,127	Johnson & Johnson	1.2	1,880	2,060
79,034,713	Kraft Foods Inc.	4.5	2,589	2,953
20,060,390	Munich Re	11.3	2,990	2,464
3,947,555	POSCO	5.1	768	1,301
72,391,036	The Procter & Gamble Company	2.6	464	4,829
25,848,838	Sanofi	1.9	2,055	1,900
291,577,428	Tesco plc	3.6	1,719	1,827
78,060,769	U.S Bancorp	4.1	2,401	2,112
39,037,142	Wal-Mart Stores, Inc.	1.1	1,893	2,333
400,015,828	Wells Fargo & Company	7.6	9,086	11,024
	Others		6,895	9,171
	Total Common Stocks Carried at market		$48,209	$76,991

*This is our actual purchase price and also out tax basis; GAAP "cost" differs in a few cases because of write-ups or write-downs that have been required.

We made few changes in our investment holdings during 2011. But three moves were important: our purchases of IBM and Bank of America and the $1 billion addition we made to our Wells Fargo position.

Source: © Berkshire Hathaway

Figure 1.16: List of most popular stocks for hedge fund managers

Exhibit 22:

POPULARITY: 50 stocks with the largest NUMBER of hedge fund investors

Company	Ticker	Sub-sector	Equity Cap ($ mil)	POPULARITY Number of Hedge Funds Owning Stock 31-Dec-11	CONCENTRATION Percent of Equity Cap owned by Hedge Funds 30-Sep-11	31-Dec-11	Chg	Total Return YTD	Short Interest as % of Mkt Cap	Avg Days Volume to Liquidate HF Position
Apple Inc.	AAPL	Computer Hardware	$464,013	216	4%	4%	0%	23%	1%	2
Google Inc. Cl A	GOOG	Internet Software & Services	156,211	172	4	5	1	(6)	2	4
Microsoft Corp.	MSFT	Systems Software	252,143	157	2	2	(0)	17	1	3
JPMorgan Chase & Co.	JPM	Other Diversified Financial Services	142,111	133	3	3	0	13	1	3
Citigroup Inc.	C	Other Diversified Financial Services	92,746	128	5	5	(1)	21	1	3
QUALCOMM Inc.	QCOM	Communications Equipment	104,158	120	4	4	(0)	13	1	4
Bank of America Corp.	BAC	Other Diversified Financial Services	78,845	107	2	2	0	40	2	1
Pfizer Inc.	PFE	Pharmaceuticals	162,272	107	2	2	(1)	(1)	1	3
Oracle Corp.	ORCL	Systems Software	140,623	104	1	1	0	9	0	2
Cisco Systems Inc.	CSCO	Communications Equipment	107,033	101	2	1	(0)	10	1	1
Yahoo! Inc.	YHOO	Internet Software & Services	18,753	99	11	13	2	(6)	3	6
Anadarko Petroleum Corp.	APC	Oil & Gas Exploration & Production	43,578	98	9	8	(1)	15	1	10
Wells Fargo & Co.	WFC	Diversified Banks	159,102	97	2	2	(1)	10	1	2
EMC Corp.	EMC	Computer Storage & Peripherals	54,623	91	3	3	0	24	5	3
Halliburton Co.	HAL	Oil & Gas Equipment & Services	32,417	90	3	5	1	2	2	3
Amazon.com Inc.	AMZN	Internet Retail	83,946	90	3	3	(0)	7	2	2
Hewlett-Packard Co.	HPQ	Computer Hardware	57,551	86	4	4	(1)	13	1	3
Express Scripts Inc.	ESRX	Health Care Services	25,275	85	13	15	1	16	17	10
Johnson & Johnson	JNJ	Pharmaceuticals	176,549	85	1	1	(0)	(1)	1	1
General Motors Co.	GM	Automobile Manufacturers	39,005	85	5	5	(0)	23	3	6
Visa Inc.	V	Data Processing & Outsourced Services	60,462	82	7	6	(0)	14	1	6
El Paso Corp.	EP	Oil & Gas Storage & Transportation	21,038	81	19	27	8	2	1	19
Exxon Mobil Corp.	XOM	Integrated Oil & Gas	403,205	81	1	1	(0)	(0)	1	1
Medco Health Solutions Inc.	MHS	Health Care Services	24,546	80	12	14	2	13	1	12
MasterCard Inc. Cl A	MA	Data Processing & Outsourced Services	47,791	78	4	4	1	5	1	5
Wal-Mart Stores Inc.	WMT	Hypermarkets & Super Centers	211,509	79	1	1	(0)	3	1	2
Occidental Petroleum Corp.	OXY	Integrated Oil & Gas	84,231	78	1	2	0	11	1	3
Merck & Co Inc	MRK	Pharmaceuticals	115,882	78	1	1	0	1	1	2
BP PLC ADS	BP	Integrated Oil & Gas	145,364	77	2	2	0	9	0	8
Chevron Corp.	CVX	Integrated Oil & Gas	209,106	77	1	1	0	(1)	1	1
Target Corp.	TGT	General Merchandise Stores	34,795	77	4	3	(1)	2	1	3
CVS Caremark Corp.	CVS	Drug Retail	66,502	76	4	3	(0)	7	1	5
WellPoint Inc.	WLP	Managed Health Care	22,663	76	7	7	(1)	(2)	2	7
Goodrich Corp.	GR	Aerospace & Defense	15,800	74	21	30	9	2	1	21
Intel Corp.	INTC	Semiconductors	135,345	74	1	1	0	10	2	1
LyondellBasell Industries N.V. Cl A	LYB	Specialty Chemicals	25,153	74	40	40	(0)	34	1	48
Corning Inc.	GLW	Electronic Components	20,527	74	5	4	(1)	4	1	3
Comcast Corp. Cl A	CMCSA	Cable & Satellite	59,680	74	4	3	(1)	20	1	3
Williams Companies Inc	WMB	Oil & Gas Storage & Transportation	17,075	74	21	15	(7)	7	3	10
Freeport-McMoRan Copper & Gc	FCX	Diversified Metals & Mining	40,191	73	3	3	(1)	16	2	1
International Business Machines	IBM	IT Consulting & Other Services	223,010	72	1	1	0	5	1	1
Schlumberger Ltd.	SLB	Oil & Gas Equipment & Services	103,221	72	2	1	(1)	13	1	2
priceline.com Inc.	PCLN	Internet Retail	28,391	71	13	16	3	22	7	7
General Electric Co.	GE	Industrial Conglomerates	198,056	71	1	1	(0)	5	1	1
Barrick Gold Corp.	ABX	Gold	47,450	71	2	2	(0)	5	1	3
News Corp. Cl A	NWSA	Movies & Entertainment	31,567	71	14	13	(0)	6	2	10
Ford Motor Co.	F	Automobile Manufacturers	46,168	71	2	2	(0)	16	3	1
Lowe's Cos.	LOW	Home Improvement Retail	34,358	71	7	6	(1)	9	2	5
Abbott Laboratories	ABT	Pharmaceuticals	86,395	70	1	1	0	(1)	1	2
Las Vegas Sands Corp.	LVS	Casinos & Gaming	38,087	70	5	5	0	22	1	2
Average			$99,570	90	6%	6%	0%	10%	2%	5
Median			60,071	79	4	3	(0)	9	1	3

Note: Based on analysis of 674 hedge funds with $704 billion of single-stock equity assets.
Holdings as of December 31, 2011; Pricing as of February 15, 2012.

Source: Lionshare via FactSet, IDC, and Goldman Sachs Global ECS Research.

How professional does this make winning spread bettors?

In 2005 money managers earned a fortune. Never in the history of economic endeavour had so much been earned by so few so quickly. They were led by Long Island fund manager James Simons of Renaissance Technologies who earned $1.5 billion, followed by T. Boone Pickens Jr. of Texas with $1.4 billion and New York investor George Soros with $840 million.

Such fortunes did not end with the credit crunch. Indeed, US hedge fund billionaire John Paulson was his industry's biggest earner in 2007, thanks to a bet against sub-prime mortgages that netted him $3.7bn in personal profit according to *Alpha Magazine*:

So what is the attitude of winning spread bettors – can they go from managing their own monies to running funds like these hedge fund giants?

Our research found that winning traders had, above all else, simplicity and consistency in their approach. Losers would tend to be complicated and/or inconsistent. We explain more below.

Do you have to trade full-time?

Our data showed that some of the most profitable traders who made money were not necessarily full time traders. They were, for instance, shopkeepers and IT managers. What the winners had in common was that they ensured the time they could extract from their day jobs fitted their form of analysis of the markets. Surprisingly they would not just use, for instance, one hour duration price charts if they knew the time they would get to examine the markets would be limited, but they would be well informed on the economic news, especially if they were trading foreign exchange.

They exemplified a clear intention to trade, and ensured, come what may, trading and systematic analysis fitted into work. They were not dabblers. Every day they monitored the markets without fail. And they were trading with meaningful sums, which meant that when we interviewed them, they were clear that this was something they expected to succeed at. They would adopt a consistent, not an opportunistic, approach and valued their returns based on the time spent. And a full-time job certainly did not prohibit them from trading.

One interviewee, who had a full-time job in the City (not a trading related job), said:

> "I made over £20k last year even though it was my first year trading. That's slightly over a 30% return for the money I had set aside for trading. Actually I didn't fund my account fully because spread betting is margined, but the most I was prepared to lose, even though not in my spread betting account, was mentally set aside."

But can such spread betting traders make big money over time?

Obviously, you must expect to have down days, months and even years, but an annual return of 33% over ten years can turn $100k into $1.7m – as the following table shows.

Figure 1.17: $100k to $1.7m

End of Year	33% return per annum
1	$133,000
2	$169,000
3	$224,770
4	$298,944
5	$397,595
6	$528,802
7	$703,306
8	$935,398
9	$1,244,079
10	$1,654,625

Forecasting the markets

Capital and labour

Making money is and will always be about compounding your time and your capital. You only have two things worth anything – capital and labour. Those without capital have to deploy labour. Anyone who has given any thought to this matter knows that deploying capital is better than deploying labour.

Trading and investing is of course about making money. But it is about how much money and how quickly and how much time you spend on making those returns.

A quantitative hedge fund which uses purely mathematical models and inputs trades to a brokerage system can generate 20% per annum return on capital with negligible time.

It is **return on time** that we are interested in.

The reason is that if you are a professional investor then you could use the time to generate additional funds and improve your business returns.

So how do we forecast with minimal time involvement?

It is more about what we do not look at, than what we do look at and, importantly, understand that complexity is not a necessary precondition to forecasting accuracy.

We found winners, as a whole, exemplified certain key criteria for forecasting prices and these are:

1.　The method needs to be **simple**.

2.　It needs to be **time efficient**.

3.　It must be able to **use technological power** to scan thousands of stocks.

4.　The method must have logical reasons why it works – it must **make sense**.

More information does not mean more accuracy – some were happy to ignore large chunks of newsflow, though this was rare.

We showed winners the income statement for US Steel, to determine how many would use any aspects of the data in their trading. Not one winning spread bettor in our sample felt they would find examining such a statement useful. Some of the responses given included:

> *"This is fine, but I wouldn't know where to get it from."*

"This is not important for the time frame I trade."

"This is too complicated. I'm a simple man, and I am making money."

"I have something that works. Why would I change it for something which looks like I'll have to go back to school?"

Technology does save time

If these winning spread bettors wanted to make money but keep their day jobs, what kinds of tools were they using? And was there a difference to what losers were using?

As a general rule, we did not find winners had some special technological knowledge over losers. But we *did* find that some winners were very well informed about online tools and had found their favourites and applied them. In the case of some, they knew the kind of tools they were looking for to make their lives easier and in the case of others it was that they came across the tool and then worked out how to make a profitable system from it.

The simplest online use of technology was the monitoring of stocks in the news. Traders would reason these would be stocks "in play" and so would be volatile and with momentum over the next few days.

But we also found those who found their buys through observation. One trader said:

> "I visit the Apple store and see how busy it is. It gives me a pretty good insight when on a Friday night many people, from children to grandparents are in there, and all the stores around don't have one tenth the customers. Then I want Apple shares."

Another trader said:

> "I love the free Google Finance Stock Screener."
> **www.google.com/finance/stockscreener**

> "There was a time, not so long ago, when technology like this cost you a fortune. You can select from more than 500 factors to quickly create a list of companies that meet your criteria, or if you'd rather, you can use all of the above pre-selected."

> Another great online tool is,
> **www.zignals.com/main/stock_screener/stock_screener.aspx.**

The most complicated system we saw from a winner was the use of very complex Elliott Wave software.

Company analysis?

> ## Tip: You don't need to care what the company does

To us a company generates numbers. That is all it does. We do not care what the company makes. We do not care about anything other than the above numbers. We found winning spread bettors were divided on this approach, but some winners certainly didn't know or care what some companies did.

1. We do not care what the company does.

2. We do not care whether it is in a good or bad sector.

3. We do not care about its competitors.

4. We do not care about news about the company.

5. We do not care about directors buying.

The upshot to this is that a company is only figures (revenues, profits, profit margins, etc.). Therefore we can *datamine* the company numbers using the web or software, without my having to read the numbers in the tables or understanding what the company does. That datamining, which looks for the figures hiding in the table, will throw up only the best companies. The trick is to know what to datamine and what tools help you do it.

This saves a lot of time – because the datamining is done by software or websites. We are not assuming that other methods of analysis do not generate returns, or that they do not generate superior returns, but this works for us.

Finding value: pragmatic analysis

So, if we are going to save time by datamining and screening, what are the key methods for finding value stocks?

One spread bettor used a free tool we particularly liked: **screener.finance.yahoo.com/presetscreens.html**

This enables you to have set preset screens that will do all the work. You can search for the following:

1. Strong forecast growth

Stocks of companies that have the highest dividend yields are often considered the index's most undervalued stocks because their prices are low relative to their dividends.

2. Large cap growth

Stocks of companies with market caps greater than $5 billion that are expected to grow earnings at least 20% next year but have price/earnings ratios of less than 20 and price/sales ratios of less than 1.5.

3. Contrarian strategy

This approach is based on the idea that the market will eventually rediscover out-of-favour stocks and bring the high-flyers back down. It looks for medium to large-cap stocks with low price/earnings ratios and a potentially strong financial condition.

4. Bargain growth

This screen, based on the so-called "growth at a reasonable price" approach, focuses on finding opportunities with modest risk in smaller capitalisation stocks.

5. Small cap growth

This screen is biased toward smaller companies and looks across all sectors for beaten-up stocks with a lot of potential growth ahead. The screen may be particularly useful for value investors.

6. Bottom fishing

Companies that appear undervalued, are profitable and have relatively low debt, but that are also fast growing and have begun to see significant stock price appreciation — making them "rockets".

7. Dogs of the Dow

This simple but effective value screen presents a pure yield play. In the remainder of the book, we examine other winning ways other spread bettors used.

Summary

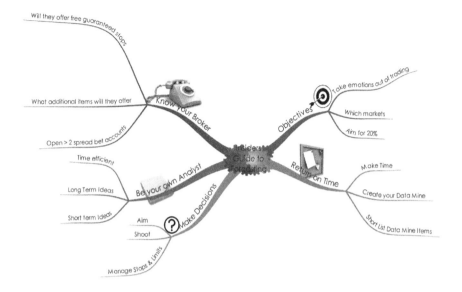

© **Paresh Kiri**

Chapter 2

Winners Use Less Financial Information

"In the acquire-or-be-acquired corporate mayhem of the 1980s, the mantle of management has passed to investment bankers and number-crunchers whose vision extends no further than the next quarterly earnings statement."

– Charles Fontaine

Introduction

- Were winning spread bettors more financially astute and educated than losers?

- Did winners have more time and relevant qualifications to understand financial data?

- Did winners use certain kinds of financial data?

You can ignore the analysts and be a good forecaster and make money

It seems winning spread betting traders know that analysts recommendations are of limited value. The way some did use them seemed markedly different to losing traders in our research. First, the winners who did use analysts reports tended to incorporate them in a broader number of factors. However, losers tended to place more weight on analysts' comments and in, some cases, used them as their trigger point for trades.

In 2000, at the height of the dot-com boom, there were 28,000 recommendations by brokerage-house analysts. As of the start of October 2001, 99.1% of those recommendations on US companies were either strong buy, buy, or hold. Just 0.9% of the time, analysts said sell.

Analysts are simple creatures to understand on television...until they open their mouths. From my (Alpesh) years on Bloomberg TV or on the BBC or interviews on Sky TV, I cannot recall a single analyst who did not like the stock he was speaking about. Worse still, when I interviewed them about this the common theme, no matter how you couch it, always seemed to be that in the long term they were positive and in the short term 'they saw market volatility.'

What they meant was:

> "In the short term it will go up and down and not the direction I am saying, so I don't want to be embarrassed if you call me back in six months because I may still be in this job at this bank. In the long term, heck all stocks go up don't they? And anyway, who's going to remember in the long term anything I say?"

In *Conflict of Interest and the Credibility of Underwriter Analyst Recommendations* authors Roni Michaely of Cornell University and Kent Womack of Dartmouth College reveal:

> "Brokerage analysts frequently comment on and sometimes recommend companies that their firms have recently taken public. We show that stocks that underwriter analysts recommend perform more poorly than buy recommendations by unaffiliated brokers prior to, at the time of, and subsequent to the recommendation date. We conclude that the recommendations by underwriter analysts show significant evidence of bias. We show also that the market does not recognize the full extent of this bias. The results suggest a potential conflict of interest inherent in the different functions that investment bankers perform."

There is a lot more conflicts of interest than you think

Investment banks traditionally have had three main sources of income:

1. corporate financing, the issuance of securities, and merger advisory services,

2. brokerage services, and

3. proprietary trading.

These three income sources may create conflicts of interest within the bank and with its clients. A firm's proprietary trading activities, for example, can conflict with its fiduciary responsibility to obtain best execution for clients.

As the above authors explain:

> "A more frequent and more observable conflict occurs between a bank's corporate finance arm and its brokerage operation. The corporate finance division of the bank is responsible primarily for completing

transactions such as initial public offerings (IPOs), seasoned equity offerings, and mergers for new and current clients. The brokerage operation and its equity research department, on the other hand, are motivated to maximise commissions and spreads by providing timely, high-quality (and presumably unbiased) information for their clients. These two objectives may conflict."

But conflict is rife:

"Many reports in the financial press also suggest that conflict of interest in the investment banking industry may be an important issue. One source of conflict lies in the compensation structure for equity research analysts. It is common for a significant portion of the research analyst's compensation to be determined by the analyst's "helpfulness" to the corporate finance professionals and their financing efforts (See, for example, *The Wall Street Journal,* June 19 1997: "All Star Analysts 1997 Survey.")"

"At the same time, analysts' external reputations depend at least partially on the quality of their recommendations. And, this external reputation is the other significant factor in their compensation. When analysts issue opinions and recommendations about firms that have business dealings with their corporate finance divisions, this conflict may result in recommendations and opinions that are positively biased."

Winners used a different kind of financial information

Many consistently winning spread bettors we spoke to did not follow the picks of others, but rather followed their historic actions. In other words: actions speak louder than words. One showed us the image below as an example of this type of financial information that they would use.

Figure 2.1: Seasonality analysis for Japanese Yen

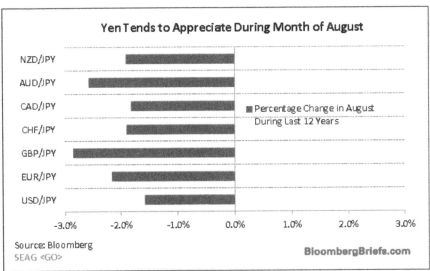

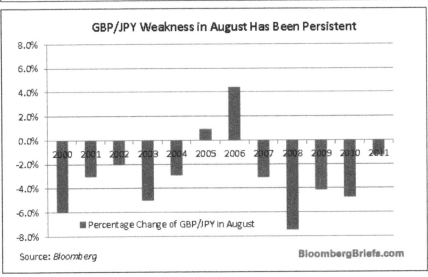

Figure 2.2: Seasonality analysis for Asian equity markets

	JAN	FEB	MAR	APR	MAY	JUN	JUL	AUG	SEP	OCT	NOV	DEC
Australia	-3.2	-0.7	2.0	1.9	-3.4	-1.7	-0.1	1.4	-0.2	-0.4	-3.1	0.3
South Korea	-1.2	-1.6	6.1	5.7	-2.7	-1.7	4.9	-4.1	2.4	-2.6	-2.8	3.8
Japan	-2.6	1.8	-0.9	2.9	-2.5	-1.3	-0.4	-4.4	-3.4	-4.7	-2.9	2.4
China	-5.6	2.8	1.1	6.1	-1.4	-0.2	5.4	-4.1	-1.5	3.7	-3.4	1.7
Indonesia	-2.5	0.1	5.2	4.3	-0.6	1.9	7.6	-3.8	0.7	-1.6	-1.3	5.0
Taiwan	-3.3	3.1	3.5	3.8	-0.3	-3.2	1.8	-3.4	-0.1	-1.9	-5.2	4.2
Thailand	-3.7	4.9	3.4	4.1	-0.2	1.3	3.3	-0.4	-0.7	-3.1	-2.1	5.5
Malaysia	-0.5	0.0	-0.1	2.6	0.1	-0.1	2.2	-3.2	-0.3	1.0	-0.8	2.5
Singapore	-2.1	-1.5	3.0	4.0	1.0	-1.2	4.5	-5.2	-0.7	-3.7	-2.3	1.3
India	-4.1	-1.1	2.6	5.4	2.0	-2.8	3.2	-1.7	4.1	-1.5	-3.4	3.5
Philippines	-3.8	0.9	3.1	1.3	2.1	-0.7	4.7	-0.1	1.4	-1.5	-3.7	1.9
AVERAGE	-3.0	0.8	2.6	3.8	-0.5	-0.9	3.4	-2.6	0.1	-1.5	-2.8	2.9

May Selling Typically Brings Summer Stalemate

SEASONAL HEAT MAP - MoM Percent Change in MSCI Equity Index

Source: *Bloomberg*

BloombergBriefs.com

Winners were efficient

We found winners had found ways of being efficient in their trading activities. After all, with a portfolio of 15 stocks, and rejecting as many companies as you accept after your research, you could easily expend 30 hours in research. Undertake the research task only four times a year and a $20,000 portfolio achieving a 15% return only carries a $25 per hour salary.

Efficiency means starting with research tasks which take the least time per company, so you can rapidly narrow down the number of possible interesting companies and spend increasing research time on the best candidates for inclusion in your portfolio.

Being your own analyst requires mimicking their efficient research routine. First, produce a list of, say, 30 stocks for further research using an online stock screen or independent stock research site. A value investor will, for instance, narrow their search according to valuation measures such as price-earnings ratios.

Second, an analyst's database of corporate history can be substituted by using the search facility on news and commentary sites to discover any problems about the company and whether it warrants exclusion from your list.

Third, fundamental data on a company for more detailed research to ensure the stocks meet your (value, growth, recovery) criteria is not the exclusive remit of the analyst but available freely.

Next, find out what the company you are researching is saying about itself. You don't need an analyst's report to access the company's annual report. Neither are analysts reports needed any longer to provide access to company conference calls or webcasts.

If small companies are your main interest then big bank analysts reports are of little use anyway because they rarely cover such companies. Small company research sites provide an alternative.

Finally, having bought the stock, monitor your holding using real time quotes and online portfolio managers – something an analyst doesn't do for you.

Winners put a lot less weight on analysts buy and sell recommendations

Of the sample group of winner and loser spread betting traders we interviewed, winners put far less weight upon analysts' forecasts than losers. It was almost as if losers lacked confidence and were more readily swayed by views of others.

A study conducted by academics found that the average annual returns of the independents' buy recommendations outpaced all the investment banks in the study by about eight percentage points a year during a prolonged time period. The study looked at how stocks performed from February 1996 through June 2003.

Some of the largest investment firms — which include Merrill Lynch & Co., Morgan Stanley and Citigroup's Smith Barney unit — are now required to provide their clients with an independent source of research in addition to their own analysts' reports.

Based on the study, when there's a conflict investors,

> "would do better by following the recommendations of the independent research providers,"

says Brett Trueman, a professor of accounting at UCLA's Anderson Graduate School of Management, who co-authored the study with Brad Barber of the University of California, Davis, and Reuven Lehavy of the University of Michigan.

According to the *Wall Street Journal,*

> "the independents' edge was particularly striking after the Nasdaq Stock Market peaked in March 2000. "During the bear market, the independents slaughtered the investment banks," says Prof. Trueman. The authors think the banks' performance had to do with the fact that they were reluctant to downgrade stocks because of investment-banking ties.
>
> The study wasn't all bad news for major brokerage firms. All of the firms in the study and the independents did just about equally well during the bull market, the study found. The authors say that's not surprising because the banks were issuing "buys" at a time when shares were largely rising.
>
> According to the study, the 10 investment banks that were part of the securities settlement turned in their worst performance between March 11, 2000, and June 2003, when stocks were performing poorly. The banks' picks underperformed those of the independents by an average of 18 percentage points a year during that period. The banks' track record was even worse for recommendations issued or outstanding after an initial public offering or follow-on stock offering during that period: Those picks underperformed by an average of 21 percentage points a year. The poor performance extended to firms with investment-banking business that weren't included in the settlement. (Under an agreement with Thomson Financial First Call, a unit of Thomson Corp. that provided the study's data, the authors agreed not to provide information about specific firms that they studied.)
>
> The study doesn't directly answer investors' questions about how good the new research will be. That's because many of the firms that will provide research under the settlement aren't in the study. Among those that are: Buckingham Research Group, Cathay Financial and Green Street Advisors Inc.
>
> Still, the findings suggest that it can pay to ask for a second opinion — and to carefully consider its findings. "The research reports investors will be getting can be quite useful supplementary information," says Prof. Trueman, who along with his colleagues looked at roughly 335,000 stock recommendations made by more than 400 securities firms."

The truth about how much data is useless and what makes money

Switch on Bloomberg, or buy a textbook on valuation analysis, and you will see a lot of figures about the types of things listed below. Under the principle of Pragmatic Analysis we do not need to know most of the information here. But we do want to take you through it. We want to take you through it because:

1. We want you to know we have not ignored it.

2. We want you to know we am not ignorant of substantial detail.

3. We want you to know we have done a trade-off between immense detail and return – that we are getting a return despite not doing hours of immense research.

4. We want you to know that the trade-off does not lead to poorer performance.

5. We want you to know you do not need to know how the car works to be a better driver, but a great driver does have some knowledge of the things he does not need to know about a car.

This next section is that interview in our words

We thought it would be helpful to illustrate how one winning spread betting trader uses fundamental data. This next section is in our words of that interview.

Sales growth

A company can perform well over the short term with rising earnings even if sales are dropping. This can occur if profits (earnings) are being increased due to cost-cutting. However, there will come a time when costs cannot be reduced any further and decreasing sales growth feeds back into lower earnings.

> "I prefer focusing on year-on-year sales growth. Now, given that one can argue there are many many more varieties to examine which are worth examining, such as sales growth relative to the industry, I nevertheless found that in my experience the extra complexities and subtleties do not add to share price performance."

Earnings per share growth

EPS growth is a key factor feeding into company growth.

The year-to-year comparison for the most recent quarter (MRQ) represents the most up-to-date growth information available to the financial community and is always an important determinant of near-term stock-price performance. Assume that strong MRQ growth rates will be accompanied by strong stock-price performance, and vice versa. If that is not the case then examine the news reports to find out why.

> "I think the focus on earnings growth year-on-year, whilst crude and simple compared to EPS and the reasons for EPS growth etc, works as a good solid component for predicting share price. Anything more complex around EPS suffers from two key problems:
>
> > **1.** the rest of the market which could move the share price does not look at it, or at least closely enough, and
> >
> > **2.** until it manifests itself in earnings growth the share price does not move anyway."

Price to earnings

The P/E ratio shows you the multiple you're paying for each dollar of earnings of the company. One would normally prefer a company with a lower P/E to one with higher a P/E. However, note that there can be little wrong with paying a higher P/E multiple for a rapidly growing company because you expect its future earnings rate to be higher.

A good rule of thumb is that a stock is attractive if its P/E ratio is lower than its long-term compound growth rate in EPS. Conversely, a company with a low P/E ratio is not necessarily a good thing. It may be because its outlook is more uncertain due to factors such as competition, a lawsuit, or a cyclical downturn.

> "I tend to look for P/E lower than the industry average."

As well as P/E, examining other similar ratios is always very useful; these are price to sales (which is especially useful for early-stage growth companies that might not have reached profitability), price to book value, and price to cash flow.

> "Again, I have found in simplicity outstanding returns. I know that by not comparing P/E to industry or changing for market climate I may miss many good stocks, but I am not trying to pick every great stock, only so many that may on average in a portfolio beat just about

everyone else on the block and to this end a simple examination for P/E of 5-25 works well in ensuring poor quality stocks are weeded out."

Beta

Beta measures stock price volatility relative to the overall stock market. So, for instance, if we use the S&P 500 as a proxy for the market as a whole and we automatically define its beta as being 1.00, then a higher beta indicates that a stock is more volatile while a lower beta indicates stability. For example, a stock with a beta of 0.90 would, on average, be expected to rise or fall only 90% as much as the market. So if the market dropped 10%, such a stock might rise or fall 9%.

"I tend to ignore individual stock beta."

Price to sales

Price to sales is generally used to evaluate companies that don't have earnings and that don't pay dividends – in recent times that has often meant internet companies. For these companies you may consider that high multiples of sales and high growth rates suggest optimistic future earnings expectations on the part of investors. Where earnings have wild swings in any particular year, for instance due to one-off items, price to sales can be a good indicator of the underlying health of the company.

"My view is keep it simple and stick to P/E. It's more than good enough and most of the important research on stock performance is based on P/E not P/S."

Price to book

Price to book is a theoretical comparison of the value of the company's stock to the value of the assets it owns (free and clear of debt). This is probably of less importance in practice than in theory. The idea behind it is that book value is a proxy for the proceeds that would be realised if the company was to be liquidated by selling all its assets and paying all its debt.

In reality, though, assets are valued on the books at the actual prices the company paid to acquire them, minus cumulative depreciation/amortization charges. The idea behind these costs is gradually to reduce the value of the assets to zero over a period of use in which they approach obsolescence.

"All in all, I tend to ignore this."

Cash flow and net income

Net income gives us some idea of how much money the company is generating, which in turn may give us an idea of the health and wealth of the company. To calculate net income, we subtract all expenses from revenues.

Unfortunately, things are never quite that simple!

For instance, a manufacturing firm spends $10 million to build a factory that will help it create products for a period of ten years. We would recognize factory construction expenses of $10 million in year one, and zero in each of years two to ten. This would suggest one unusually poor year for profits, followed by nine very good ones.

The preferred practice is to match revenues as closely as possible to the expenses incurred to generate those revenues. In our example, we assume that the $10 million factory generates ten years' worth of revenues so we apportion one-tenth of the $10 million outlay in each of those ten years. This one-tenth charge is known as depreciation (amortization is a similar annual charge for a different sort of one-off expenditure that is matched against more than one year's worth of sales).

But cash flow alone doesn't give us the full story. *Free cash flow* looks at the cash the company's operations actually generated in a given year and subtracts important 'non-operating' cash outlays, capital spending and dividend payments. Accordingly, free cash flow is the purest measure of a company's capacity to generate cash.

Cash flow is a less pure number, but also less susceptible to wide year-to-year swings as capital programmes periodically build up and wind down.

Clearly, we are looking to compare price to cash flow and price to free cash flow relative to other companies in the same industry and also to see how cash flow and free cash flow change year on year for the company in order to gauge a measure of its growth and valuation. We want price to cash flow ratios to be low relative to other companies in the same industry and we want cash flow to be rising year on year.

> "Again, whilst cash flow is important, I tend to judge growth by growth in earnings and sales."

Dividend information

The annual dividend is the total amount of dividends you could expect to receive if you held the stock for a year and there was no change in the company's dividend payment. It is based on the current quarterly dividend payment rate projected forward for four quarters. Since I look for growth companies I prefer it if the company reinvests its dividend rather than paying it to shareholders.

There was a time when a company not paying a dividend could expect to have its share price punished by virtue of the fact that many conservative funds looking for income rather than capital growth from their stocks would steer clear of such companies. Higher yields on stocks can suggest Wall Street expectations of sluggish growth.

The *dividend yield* is the indicated annual dividend rate expressed as a percentage of the price of the stock, and could be compared to the coupon yield on a bond. It allows you to see how much income you can expect per $ or £ investment from this stock, so allowing you to compare it with other stocks you may be looking at. Some prefer high yield, others low. If you are looking for high growth companies as a general rule, all other things being equal, you will prefer low yield companies.

The *payout ratio* tells you what percentage of the company's earnings have been given to shareholders as cash dividends over the past twelve months. I look for stocks with a low payout ratio, which indicates that the company has chosen to reinvest most of the profits back into the business.

There are a few sectors whose stocks are regarded as income vehicles – utility and real estate in particular. Investors in these sectors focus more on yields than those in other sectors.

> "For me, I like dividend yielding companies because not only do I have a downside protection against share price moves in the form of dividends, but also if the price falls, then the stock tends to be more attractive because its yield has just improved so others rush in to buy the stock and prevent it falling too much."

Return on equity

The shareholders of a company can be thought of as having given a company capital – or equity. The return on equity (ROE) is a measure of how effectively the company has managed this equity. Equity represents that portion of the company's assets that would be distributed to shareholders if the company were liquidated and all assets sold at values reflected on the company's balance sheet, so it is what the company itself and therefore the shareholders own and does not include, for instance, money loaned from a bank.

> "Whilst this is popular with many investors – again, I find a better measure of whether a company share price will rise is its valuation and growth."

Return on investment

Since return on investment (ROI) only relates to capital provided by shareholders, it is a limited measure of management effectiveness since we also want to know how the company is performing with the other sources of money at its disposal. Return on investment shows how effective management is in utilising money provided by the company's owners (equity) and long-term creditors.

> "I don't think this helps me getting it right."

Return on assets

As well as shareholder capital and long-term money granted to the company there are also shorter-term loans of capital, and so return on assets (ROA) is a broader measure than the above two of how a company is handling funds provided to it. For example, an internet company may borrow money to purchase some Sun Microsystems routers for its website. The lender may be providing short-term (i.e. less than one year) credit. Return on assets measures management's effectiveness in using everything at its disposal (equity, long-term credit and temporary capital) to produce profits.

> "Yes, one can see this is a sensible measure and how it can help in forecasting – but I don't use it. Why? It complicates, it does not add forecasting accuracy."

Profitability

Profitability ratios relate to how much of the revenue the company receives is being turned into profit.

Gross margin shows you what percentage of each revenue dollar is left after deducting direct costs of producing the goods or services which in turn bring in the revenue. For a services company, the most common direct costs would be the salaries of its employees.

The money left at this stage is called *gross profit*. Gross margin expresses the relationship between gross profit and revenues in percentage terms. For example, a gross margin of 10% means that ten cents out of every revenue dollar are left after deducting direct costs.

Operating profit and operating margin follow the progress of each revenue dollar to another important level. From gross profit we now subtract indirect costs, often referred to as overheads. Examples of overheads would be the costs associated with headquarters operations: costs that are essential to the business, but not directly connected to any single individual product manufactured and sold by the company.

Finally, *net profit* and the *net margin* show you how much of each revenue dollar is left after all costs, of any kind, are subtracted, such as interest on corporate debt and income taxes. High margins are better than low margins, and this applies equally when comparing companies in the same industry.

> "As mentioned, I prefer rising earnings and preferably increasing profit margins but the latter is not a dealbreaker for me."

Institutional ownership

Institutional Ownership Tables show the extent to which institutional investors (pension funds, mutual funds, insurance companies, etc.) own a stock.

Traders take account of institutional ownership for several reasons, one of which is that if the major institutions are buying, with all their high-flying analysts backing a stock and their millions of dollars vested in these companies, then perhaps we should be more assured in our own decisions.

There is also another way institutional ownership can back or provide trading ideas. If institutions that own a position in the company are small, that would indicate that the company has been noticed a little by institutions with potential for greater recognition. But the stock may rise as it gets better known and more institutions decide to buy in.

Many believe it is best to own a company that is between 5 and 20% owned by institutions. Such a level would suggest that there is some institutional interest and some knowledge of the company, and that there's also ample room for more institutional interest in the future.

> "For me institutional ownership is nice to have, but not compelling enough to be a dealbreaker."

Insider trading

Who knows a company even better than institutions? Maybe the company's executives and senior officers do. These are the insiders. If they are buying then perhaps we should be too, or at least be reassured. It's not just their buying – their level of holding can be an important sign too.

However, when insiders own a very large and controlling percentage of the company, they may not feel responsible to outside shareholders. This is particularly visible in companies with multiple classes of stock, with insiders/management retaining voting control over the company.

Insider selling can, and often does, reflect little more than a desire on the part of key employees to convert part of their compensation (e.g. stock options) to cash for other uses. So it need not automatically be bearish. However, this is what makes insider trading a difficult gauge of a good or bad stock.

But buying by insiders could be a different story. Here, people are putting new money into the stock of their corporations, and possibly reducing the diversification of their personal assets. It's highly unlikely that any insider would do this unless he/she had a favourable assessment of the company's prospects.

> "Of course insiders could be buying after a big fall in the stock price in an effort to show faith in the company – and that may be a desperate attempt to encourage outsiders to invest, who, if they do not, could mean the stock keeps falling. Also, insiders could simply be wrong in their assessment about the future prospects of the company. Ummm...think Lehman Brothers."

The winning strategy of one spread bettor using financial information and chart

Event Trading GBP/USD

Figure 2.3: GBP/USD

We know at A (i.e. 09:30) there is important economic data coming out likely to affect GBP. (We know this from the Economic Calendar on **www.dailyfx.com**.)

Now,

- at the end of minute 1, we notice the market is lower,

- so as soon as in minute 2 it breaks below the low of minute 1, we sell GBP/USD at B,

- our exit is 1 minute high, 3 minute high and 5 minute high; C is 1 minute high (i.e. the price is higher than previous minute),

- at point D it is 3 minute high.

In practice, my trades are shown below.

Figure 2.4: Trade log

Description	Action	Amount		Opened	Closed
GBPUSD - Rolling Spot	Trade Receivable		P	1.57228	1.57064
GBPUSD - Rolling Spot	Trade Receivable		P	1.57112	1.57064
GBPUSD - Rolling Spot	Trade Payable		L	1.57011	1.57064
GBPUSD - Rolling Spot	Trade Payable		L	1.57005	1.57065
GBPUSD - Rolling Spot	Trade Receivable		P	1.57074	1.57073

P = profit; L = loss.

NB: as I am in profit, and the trade goes in my direction – I add to the position.

If any of those later positions turn into losses, I exit.

I went short GBP/USD remember: sold short to open at 1.57228 and bought back to close at 1.57064 to make 164 pips profit. If I bet £1 per pip then I make £164 on that trade

Figure 2.5: Dealing screen

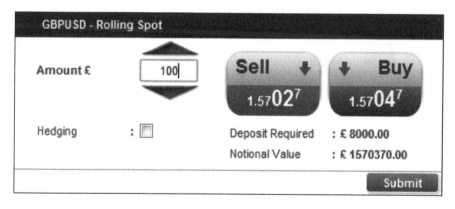

Figure 2.6: Timetable of economic data affecting the Euro

07:00		EUR German Consumer Price Index - EU Harmonised (YoY) (FEB F)	High
07:00		EUR German Consumer Price Index (YoY) (FEB F)	High
07:00		EUR German Consumer Price Index - EU Harmonised (MoM) (FEB F)	Medium
07:00		EUR German Consumer Price Index (MoM) (FEB F)	Medium
07:45		EUR French Industrial Production (MoM) (JAN)	Low
07:45		EUR French Industrial Production (YoY) (JAN)	Low
07:45		EUR French Manufacturing Production (MoM) (JAN)	Low
07:45		EUR French Manufacturing Production (YoY) (JAN)	Low
08:00		EUR German Trade Balance (euros) (JAN)	Medium
08:00		EUR German Current Account (euros) (JAN)	Low
08:00		EUR German Exports s.a. (MoM) (JAN)	Low
08:00		EUR German Imports s.a. (MoM) (JAN)	Low
08:00		EUR German Labor Costs Seas. Adj. (QoQ) (4Q)	Low
08:00		EUR German Labor Costs Workday Adj (YoY) (4Q)	Low

Source: DailyFx.com

Above is a list of times and economic data affecting the Euro and the importance of the data – i.e. how likely it is to cause the currency to move. You can see 07:00 and 08:00 are important times.

Figure 2.7: GBP/USD

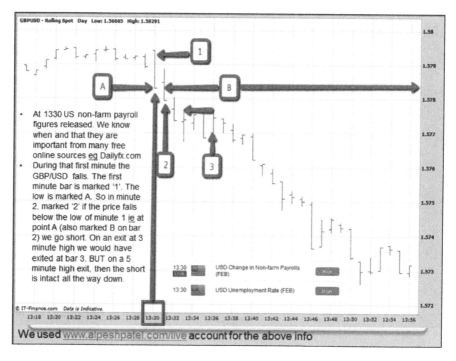

As with all event trading I like to:

1. Look at one minute charts.

2. I wait for the first minute to complete. If it is, say, down, then I go short in the second minute as soon as the low of the first minute is breached.

3. Exit 50% on a 2 minute high and 50% on a 3 minute high (i.e. the highest the price has been in 2 minutes or 3 minutes).

Figure 2.8: Discount cash flow analysis

Is Facebook really worth its IPO price?

Adjust the key assumptions in this valuation model

DCF discount rate 15%

Reset to original values

	2012-13	2018-21
Revenue growth	62%	11%
EBIT margin	30%	25%

Revenue path | Revenue/EBIT margin

● Facebook projected ● Google lagged 7yrs

$70,000

$0

2011 2012 2013 2014 2015 2016 2017 2018 2019 2020 2021

Equity DCF value

$58 billion $21.1 per share

26 32

0 25 50 75 100 125 150

■ Value from pre-2021 ☐ Post-2021

Value per active Facebook user **$64**

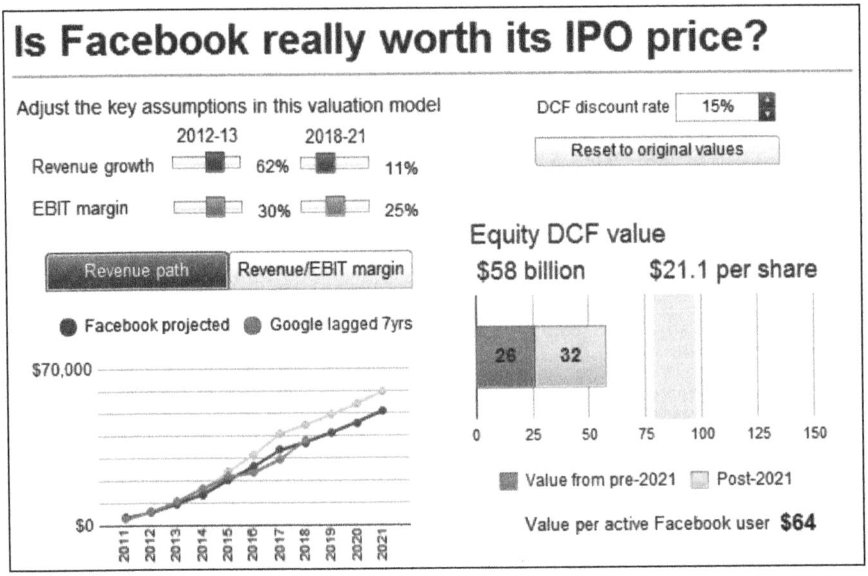

Created by Alpesh using FT.com

A rare exception

One exception to using financial data which we came across was a successful spread bettor using a lot of financial data – namely Discount Cash Flow.

Opposite is the type of analysis used to work out that Facebook was overpriced. Discount Cash Flow analysis is beyond the scope of this book, but it was interesting that it worked well for this trader to short Facebook.

Figure 2.9: Discount cash flow analysis

	2011	2012	2013	2014	2015	2016	2017	2018
Sales growth (%)	88	80	80	80	80	80	80	80
Ebitda margin (%)	50	50	50	50	50	50	50	50
Capex-to-sales ratio (%)	30	30	30	30	30	30	30	30

10-year Treasury yield (%)	2	Equity risk premium (%)	5	Beta			1.5
Cost of equity (%)	9.5	Terminal growth rate %	3	Fully diluted shares (m)			2500
		Market value ($bn)	75.5	**Share value ($)**			30.21

Created by Alpesh using FT.com

Summary

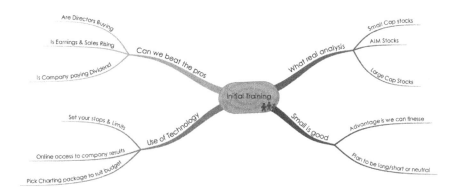

Created by Paresh Kiri

Chapter 3

Winners and News

"Every day I get up and look through the Forbes *list of the richest people in America. If I'm not there, I go to work."*

– Robert Orben

Introduction

Before we started our research on winning and losing traders, we fully expected that winners would be more glued to Bloomberg and CNBC than losers. The reasons were obvious; that winners surely were more intimate with every market move, more dedicated. And, after all, we appeared on those channels too – so surely our winning clients would be glued!

Wrong.

Whilst of course winners did watch such channels, it was clear it was not a competitive advantage or a differentiator for them as winning spread betting traders. More importantly was the reason why they did not use financial TV. Some just said they didn't have the time, but others were more forthcoming – as we reveal below.

You can always find what you want to hear from the financial media

1. Arguments for following the news

Following the news to forecast prices is good because:

1. With enough knowledge and know-how we can get a handle on the direction of the market.

2. News is attractive because people love stories.

3. News is attractive as a method of forecasting because people like to appear smart. It makes for great dinner conversation to have a theory. A view. To be educated.

Well, I was educated at Oxford University and an Oxford Don at 29, and my politics tutor told me, "don't waste your time reading *The Economist* – make your own views". News is opinion often, not fact. That may or may not move the market. But it is another layer of complexity in trying to forecast the market.

Now look at the figure below taken from Google of the chart of RIMM – the makers of Blackberry. The letters represent news items. Can you see any correlation between news and price?

Did news give us an idea where the price might go?

Figure 3.1: Share price of RIMM and news flow

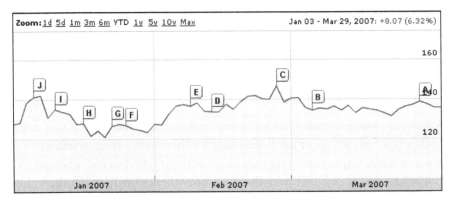

Source: Google

Figure 3.2: Index for RIMM news flow

A Research in Motion offers games
BusinessWeek - 26 Mar 2007
Ahead of the Bell: Research in Motion BusinessWeek
RIM's Crimson Tide Unstrung
HULIQ - TechNewsWorld

B RIM to Restate $250M After Options Review
InternetNews.com - 5 Mar 2007
BlackBerry-maker Research in Motion to restate results, co-
CEO... San Jose Mercury News
RIM to restate earnings by $250m Financial Times
MSN Money - InformationWeek

C Ahead of the Bell: Research in Motion
Forbes - 26 Feb 2007

D RIM to Introduce Newest BlackBerry
MSN Money - 12 Feb 2007
RIM introduces newest BlackBerry San Jose Mercury News
RIM exec doesn't see threat from Apple's iPhone
Reuters.uk
BusinessWeek - Reuters

E BlackBerry, BlackJack makers settle suit
BusinessWeek - 7 Feb 2007
RIM and Samsung settle suit over BlackJack device
Reuters
RIM Settles Samsung Suit over BlackJack Device eWeek
Bloomberg - San Jose Mercury News

F Canadian Pension Fund Seeks RIM Lawsuit
TheStreet.com - 25 Jan 2007 - Related articles »

G Ahead of the Bell: Research in Motion Up
BusinessWeek - 23 Jan 2007
UPDATE 1-RESEARCH ALERT-Needham cuts Research In
Motion to hold Reuters
Goldman says buy RIM; market listens Globe and Mail
National Post - Apple Insider

H RIM Runs Pearl White Sale
InternetNews.com - 17 Jan 2007
RIM shares sink along with Pearl prices BusinessWeek
T-Mobile and RIM Launch White BlackBerry Pearl TMCnet
Reuters - Reuters

2. Arguments against following the news

And, now, following news to forecast prices will not work because:

1. Once the news is out there, the price has moved.

2. The directional move is indeterminate. Earnings are strong, for instance, but does that mean the price will move up because they have exceeded expectations? Or does it mean the price will fall because they have not? And what were the expectations anyway? Expectations of what? Net earnings? Pre-tax before exceptionals? Earnings before interest, tax, depreciation, amortisation? Who interprets this? How can we forecast?

The market often buys on the rumour and sells on the fact. But it does not do that often enough to make it a rule. The point is, news based forecasting does not have rules, it is not systematic or process driven.

Take the RIMM example. Look at point (F) which coincides with quite a volatile period in the stock.

What do we make of this?

Is it irrelevant? Then again the price drops after the news. What of other news before then or after? Do we trade short term? How do we weigh the news? But the price rises soon after without news too.

Nassim Taleb, author of *Fooled by Randomness*, explains it best: ultimately we will not know the full story, and if we did we will interpret it using our individual rationality and logic.

Tip: Do not try to forecast based on news. It's too hit and miss, but be happy to trade using a set of rules to limit your losses.

Only listen to a CEO for reasons *not* to buy his stock

One winning spread betting trader put it best for us:

> "I look at financial news for reasons *not* to do something, not for reasons to confirm my view, but to disconfirm it."

We include below some of our own translations of CEO-speak to help you along:

CEO says	Translation
Profits are up	Profit is opinion, but cash is fact. Our profits are up even though we have less cash in the bank because we sold some of our crown jewel assets as a one off. So the profit rise is a one-off exceptional item not the start of a trend. And those assets we sold, we'll need those in the future. Actually, when we said we sold those assets, it wasn't for cash. It was a barter arrangement and ummm...so our cash balance isn't improved...but hey, we can still call it profit because we put a notional value in the accounts.
Prospects are good	We are not telling you about the contingent liabilities, the lawsuits and the pension provisions. We can lean on the accountant to say it is not too bad and so our figures don't look too bad, until the proverbial hits the fan that is. But hey, I'll have left by then.
I have every confidence in the company	That damn headhunter still hasn't agreed my golden handshake at the next job.
We have increased profits from increased revenue growth.	You might think sales are growing and this is adding to profits, especially with wider profits margins. That would get your vote. But I am afraid I am tricking you. We are counting money that is expected but not in hand. That allows us to show greater revenues and profits. Guess what? Sometimes we think there is little chance of getting that money. Bristol-Myers Squibb overstated $2.5 billion in revenues and $900 million in earnings between 1999 and 2001 by giving incentives to move product before the end of its quarters.
We have increased market share	Sounds good doesn't it. Actually this is achieved from a lower profit margin and that means price-cutting to increase volume. That can be fine in the short term, but longer term those earnings may not be regarded necessarily as high quality.
Our cost-cutting programme means our profits are up	Cost cutting can be a short-term benefit before longer term profitability is hit. Imagine for instance companies cutting on research and development. This years earnings go up, but in five years you pay the real price for potentially under-investing.
People selling our stock are misguided	Actually they're xxxxxx! In April 2000, Enron CEO called hedge fund manager Richard Grubman an a—hole during a conference call with analysts and investors. Less than eight months later, the company was filing for bankruptcy, costing investors billions.
Don't worry about the footnotes	Heck that's where I have hidden everything.
If you ignore the one-offs it looks very healthy	Yeah, these one-off expenses come in every year, they're not so one off. Cendant, Kodak, Edison International, HCA, Weyerhauser. Each of these companies took a special charge/gain in each of the 20 quarters between 1998 and 2002.
We're sorry to lose him as a director, but he'll still be a consultant	Yes, a very lucrative consulting contract indeed and I hope to get one when I leave...we're trying to make it a tradition in the boardroom.
The director did well and so we feel the perks are sound practice	Damn you're good, no one hardly ever notices the non-cash perks such as flights on the corporate jet. Of course that doesn't mean we run the company like a personal bank account....
Yes, we have increased the amount in non-audit fees we pay the accounting firm	Damn again, you really know your stuff! Okay Enron also paid a lot more to their auditors, who just happened to look the other way, but we're not playing that game.

This is why the media stops you forecasting well

Financial media is short term and it's late and it is only partially informed.

End of story.

Media unfortunately may spook you out of good long-term positions. The skill is in making sure that you spread trade the news in the short term – and invest in the markets long term. Do not mix your time frames!

One thing financial TV is great at is stuffing you full of earnings announcements. As they pontificate, trying to look all serious, as if anyone really knows what 'earnings before interest, tax, depreciation and amortization' really means, you might think profits warnings are bad.

A 'profits warning' by a company would seem to be a good reason to steer clear of its shares. After all, the subsequent price fall can be both swift and costly.

Indeed, stocks fall on average 16% on the day of a warning itself according to one study[1].

But where there's fear in the market, there's money to be made. And profit warnings are no exception.

So what should you do if you're unfortunate enough to hold shares in a company that issues a profits warning?

Buy some more it seems – but not straight away. Possibly maximise on the short term uncertainty by **going short on your spread bet platform**, while the dust settles and you can assess whether it's worth selling your actual holding. If you do this then you are hedging your cash position and giving yourself time to calmly make a more rational judgement call.

Stocks of UK companies that issued profits warnings deliver returns that are on average 22% more than the FTSE All-Share index in the year beginning *12 months after* the warning. That is the key finding of the above study.

What about the short term?

What's the best way to beat the market immediately following a profits warning? There are two opposing views.

---

[1] *Stock Returns Following Profit Warnings* by Professor George Buckley, Richard Harris, Renata Herrerias of University of Exeter presented at the Royal Economic Society's 2002 Annual Conference, 26 March 2002.

One group believes stocks will rebound after a profits warning; the other believes stocks will fall even further. Who's right and where's the money to be made?

The first group argues the market overreacts to news and so following a profit warning the market drives a share price too low in the short term. They therefore buy stocks after bad news; they are the contrarians.

The second group believes the market under-reacts to news and that it's slow to revise its existing views on a company. They buy stocks on good news on the assumption the stocks will rise even further in the short term. Conversely, they stay clear in the short-term of stocks issuing profits warnings. **My experience puts me in this group.** These are sometimes called momentum traders.

According to the study, it seems momentum traders will do better than contrarians because over the six months following a warning companies' stock prices fall on average a further 5%.

The apparent contradiction between shorter term trades and longer term investments (where following a profits warning stocks fall in the short term and rise in the long term) is supported by other studies too[2]. This study found a portfolio constructed by buying stocks which were losers in the last five years and up to one year ago is profitable, so is buying winners over the last 12 months.

> ### So in the short term steer clear of companies issuing profits warnings and get in at the start of their second year after the profits warning.

As traders we're reluctant to cut our losses, often holding on in hope of a turnaround[3]. Perhaps this is partly from the shock of a profits warning and a drop of around 16% in a day. Unfortunately, by the time we give up hope of a rise and decide to ditch the stock, it may be just about to turn around.

One note of caution: the studies were performed on a relatively narrow sample, and it seems foolhardy to purely buy stocks solely on the basis of a

---

[2] *Multifactor Explanations of Asset Pricing Anomolies* by Eugene Fama and Kenneth French 1996, Journal of Finance
[3] *Are investors reluctant to realise their losses?* Terence Odean, Journal of Finance 1998.

profits warning a year earlier. Prior to buying stocks you should still look for evidence of improved performance by the company. Nevertheless, we need not fear profit warnings as much as we might have done.

Directors' deals

Another favourite of the financial media is the company director. Surely he is a person to be trusted to understand his own company.

The theory behind directors' dealings is simple: directors should know more about their own companies than outsiders. Therefore, if the directors are buying shares this should signal the company is doing well and that the share price will rise.

But "which companies have the directors themselves been buying stock?" is the wrong question to ask. That's too simplistic.

It could also be that the share price has fallen sharply and they're buying stock as a public statement of confidence in the company. Equally, it could be part of their estate planning, tax re-organisation, or an exercise of options. These purchases are hardly calculated moves based on the director's belief in a share price rise.

An equally wrong question to ask is, "in which companies are directors selling shares?"

Wharton's Andrew Metrick and Harvard's Leslie Jeng constructed a hypothetical portfolio of all insider (the US term for high ranking corporate officers including directors) sales over a 10-year period ending in 1996. The portfolio merely performed in line with the market. You might as well have ignored directors' sales altogether.

If directors' dealings do work as a signal, they don't work in an obvious, easy or straightforward way.

Instead of asking "are the directors of this company buying or selling its stock", we should ask, "how accurate a predictor of share price movements are this director's transactions?"

> Company insiders such as directors are irrelevant to spread betting. They can't even forecast their own inventory for tomorrow, let alone profits for next quarter.

That was the strong view of one of the winning spread betting traders we spoke to.

Analysts' upgrades and downgrades

Another favourite for financial TV is the analyst. He looks so grown up, that 25-year old. This category of pundit dresses the part, uses all the rights words, 'ebitda, pre-tax, earnings enhancing, M&A, profit margins, competitor analysis' – sometimes he even uses them in the right order.

There's just one small problem: there is nothing more useless to the private investor than an analyst's stock upgrade or downgrade.

You would be wrong to think an upgrade heralds a price rise. If it were that simple why did Logica, Cable & Wireless and Vodafone all slump within six weeks of an upgrade?

Maybe the price rise comes later?

It certainly didn't when investment bank McDonald Investment upgraded Amazon to a 'strong buy' when the stock was at $70. It fell to $40 in nine months and $15 in 18 months. Just one rotten apple? There gets a point where there are so many rotten apples that the whole barrel needs dumping.

Surely upgrades can then give us an advance notice of good corporate earnings announcements? No, upgrades regularly come belatedly after bumper results. Thanks, but I know how to read bumper earnings.

What of downgrades?

Maybe they give net traders advance warning of trouble ahead? If they do, it's impossible to discern. Where were the downgrades before British American Tobacco's recent weak results (heralded with the headline 'BAT results at bottom end of forecasts')?

Sure, sometimes analysts do upgrade to a strong buy and the stock rises. But if you throw enough strong buys around some are bound to be correct.

So who follows analyst upgrades? Maybe fund managers do. After all, 82% of fund mangers failed to beat the stock market over the past 20 years according to Virgin Money.

Do the opposite of what the analysts are doing

Research[4]* shows you could forecast the earnings growth of a particular company more accurately by ignoring the analysts' forecasts; instead companies with high or low forecast growth will typically just grow at the same rate as the average company.

Bulkley and Harris show it is possible to earn excess returns by buying shares for which earnings growth is forecast to be low and holding them for five years. Over that period of time, the excessive pessimism should become apparent.

Consequently, between 1982 and 1993, you could on average have earned an excess return of 5% a year (over and above the average return on all shares) by this strategy. Over the same period, shares with the highest forecast earnings growth underperformed the market by an average of 5% a year.

Summary

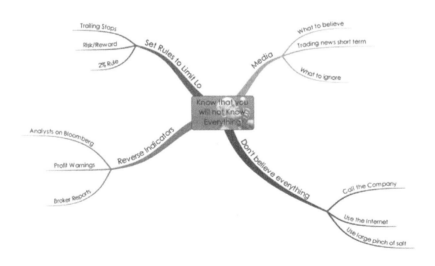

Created by Paresh Kiri

---

[4] *Irrational Analysts' Expectations as a Cause of Excess Volatility in Stock Prices* by *George Bulkley and Richard Harris, Economic Journal (March 1997).
Consistent failure to accurately predict mean earnings: An Evaluation of US Security Analysts Forecasts Working Paper, November 2001 by Ahmed El-Galfy & William Forbes.

Chapter 4

Winners Show
How to Use Charting

"There are many methods for predicting the future. For example, you can read horoscopes, tea leaves, tarot cards, or crystal balls. Collectively, these methods are known as 'nutty methods.' Or you can put well-researched facts into sophisticated computer models, more commonly referred to as 'a complete waste of time'."

– Scott Adams

Winners had a couple of strategies

From our studies we found winners tended to have one or two simple strategies which they deployed. Losers were either non-systematic and opportunistic or they tended to change and flit between an armoury of many strategies.

Winners were essentially looking at ways of knowing when to get into trends. Those that used price charts had theories they had made themselves from observation, or they applied with discipline the methods of others.

For instance, as illustrated in the following four figures, winners had an understanding of where prices close before a trend will start or change, that prices close near the high of each period when momentum is strong, and can rise but close near the low for a period when momentum is about to be lost and a trend change direction. They then use such insights to form their strategies. Strategies were always composed of simple observations and insights and then implemented with discipline.

Figure 4.1: Price closing near high for the period

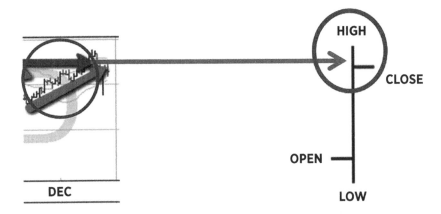

© Alpesh Patel

Figure 4.2: Prices closing near highs during an uptrend

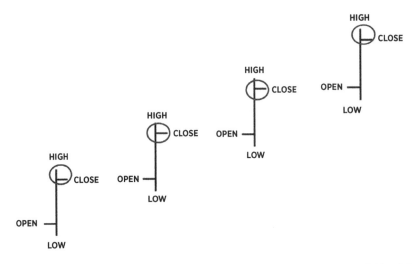

© Alpesh Patel

Figure 4.3: The highs during an uptrend

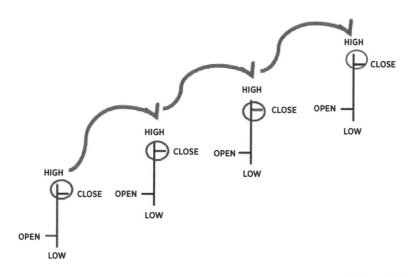

© Alpesh Patel

Figure 4.4: Price switching to closing near the low of the day

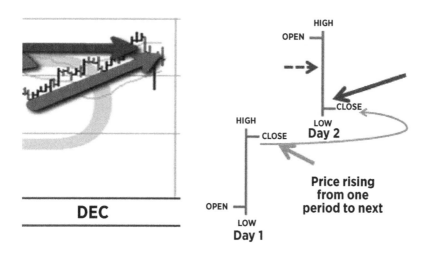

© Alpesh Patel

Strategies of winning traders all had something in common which losers did not. The winners had managed to find good timing, the remainder consistently were either entering too early or too late (see Figure 4.5).

Figure 4.5: Example of early, good and late timing

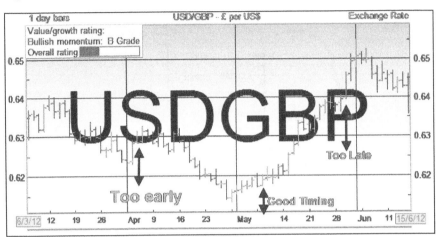

Created by Alpesh using Alpesh Patel Special Edition of Sharescope

The rewards of correct timing were clear to see for those who got it right (Figures 4.6 to 4.10).

Figure 4.6: Example of good timing

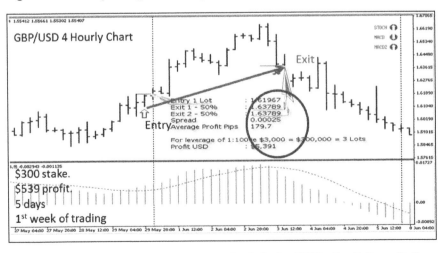

Created using MT4 Trading Software Platform

Figure 4.7: Example of good timing

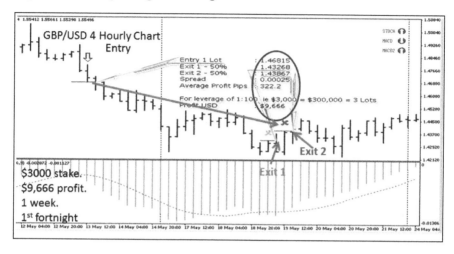

Created using MT4 Trading Software Platform

Figure 4.8: Example of good timing

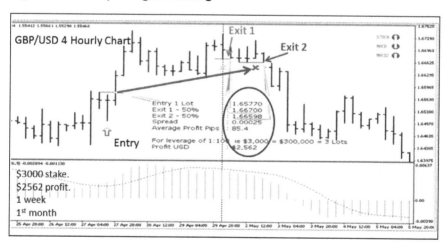

Created using MT4 Trading Software Platform

Figure 4.9: Example of good timing

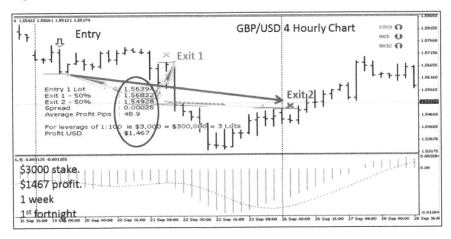

Created using MT4 Trading Software Platform

Figure 4.10: Example of correct timing

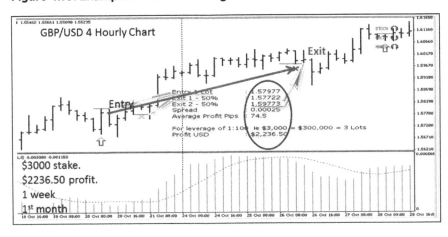

Created using MT4 Trading Software Platform

An example of one simple winning strategy deployed to great effect is shown below (we showed you this figure earlier, in the Introduction).

Figure 4.11: Analysis of the trades of a winning strategy

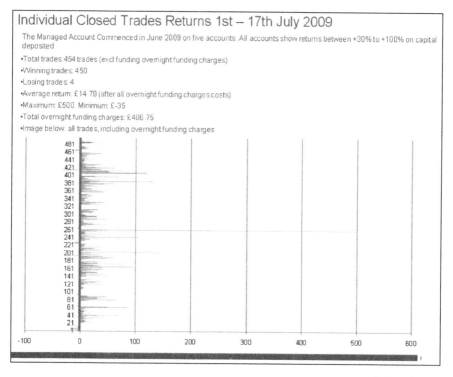

Individual Closed Trades Returns 1st – 17th July 2009

The Managed Account Commenced in June 2009 on five accounts. All accounts show returns between +30% to +100% on capital deposited

•Total trades: 454 trades (excl funding overnight funding charges)

•Winning trades: 450

•Losing trades: 4

•Average return: £14.79 (after all overnight funding charges costs)

•Maximum: £500. Minimum: £-35

•Total overnight funding charges: £406.75

•Image below: all trades, including overnight funding charges

So what was the strategy adopted to achieve this result?

The trader concerned was trading FX; he worked on the basis that FX rates move in cycles around equilibrium levels as shown in Figure 4.12 and 4.13.

Figure 4.12: FX rates moving around equilibrium levels

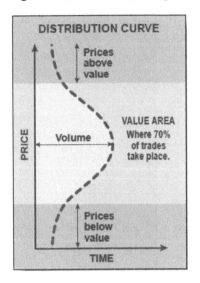

Figure 4.13: FX rates moving around equilibrium levels

So every time the price moved around a value area the trader would place a trade.

Using Figure 4.14 as an example, assume the mean reversion line is the average around which the price moves. For this spread bettor, if the price then moves to point A, he would expect it to move back to the mean reversion line. He would place a stop-loss at point B which is the distance from A to the mean reversion line, but in the opposite direction. The result: he would win 20 points by going from A to the mean reversion line, and he ensured he would not lose more than 20 points by going from A to B.

Figure 4.14: Example of rates around the Mean Reversion Line

In this example the trade narrowly misses B and goes on to hit the mean reversion at a profit at point C.

How to use price charts to make money

Our interest is not in the academic study of an infinite variety of charting techniques from the elegance of Japanese candlesticks to the maddening complexity of Elliot Waves. Our interest is to cut to the chase of how to use price charts to make money.

So let us gather some of the thoughts we have touched upon so far:

No matter which technique you use, no matter how expert you become in using it, you will only ever be right six or seven times out of ten as already explained. You can be the black belt of Elliot, the Jedi Master of Fibonacci, but you will always be somewhere between the 50-50 of a coin toss and the perfection of God.

Consequently, it's not the technique or mastery of it that matters, but that energies are spent on ensuring how to make more when chance puts you in the correct direction; then you lose when chance puts you in the wrong direction.

In this chapter we will:

1. get a primer on techniques,

2. learn some strategies, and

3. find some simple websites and software to allow us to use them.

With spread trading it's a lot simpler than the technicians would have you believe.

Why do people not make money in the markets?

Because they do the opposite of what they should.

First, they get blown out because they have a string of losing trades. Well, obviously if they bet smaller sizes they would have survived. So clearly their bet size was wrong – whether using price charts or not. Or maybe a combination of not having stops in place and hoping for a recovery.

Second, they don't know when to exit, either with a profit or a loss. It's all very well betting on the direction of the market, but for how long? When do you jump ship? The so-called experts never tell you that.

So let us.

The key is simplicity – we will cover the most basic charting signals and using either the AutoChartist function or drawing in your own analytical support and resistance you should be able to trade with confidence and know where to place your targets and your stops through the spread trading platform.

Websites taking the strain

Figure 4.15: A charting program detects price patterns

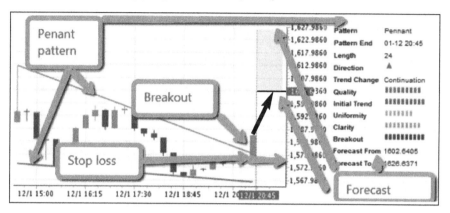

Source: www.sterlingmarkets.com

Figure 4.15 shows how a spread betting website charting program automatically detects price patterns.

The type of price breakout you see above is for Brookdale, a US stock. The reason I like this type of trade is:

1. Breakouts usually put the odds in your favour of momentum in a particular direction, in this case up, as shown by the black arrow. So you don't have to guess.

2. They let you limit your risk as you can put a stop-loss just under the breakout point, because the price should not go there if it is a proper breakout.

3. They also give you a forecast or profit target. In this case at least to 1602 and upper end to 1626.

4. So you know: entry, profit target, and risk.

5. Next you ensure the most you lose from entry to stop-loss is no more than 2% of your total trading capital. For example, if you had $10,000, you should not lose more than $200 if your stop-loss is hit.

So all the elements of a good trade are in place: odds in your favour, clear plan, limited risk.

Figure 4.16 and 4.17 shows how auto-charting facilities allow us to trade.

Figure 4.16: Auto-charting

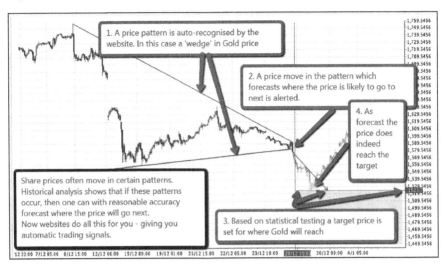

Figure 4.17: Auto-charting

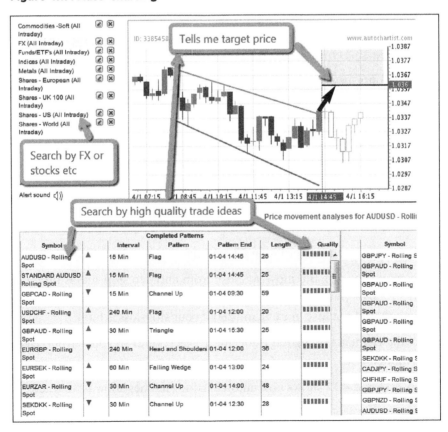

Are price charts just bunkum?

For those who think share prices are random and unpredictable, there is predictability from chaos. The movement of share prices has been described as random, chaotic, and unpredictable. But consider this experiment:

1. Place three dots at the vertices of an equilateral triangle.

2. Colour the top vertex red, the lower left one green and the lower right one blue.

3. Take a dice and colour two faces red, two faces blue and two faces green.

4. Start at any point on the paper – the Seed. Roll the dice, and whichever colour appears move the Seed half the distance towards the respective coloured vertex.

5. Repeat this. Do not plot the first 15 points generated. Then start recording them.

Figure 4.18: Predictability from chaos

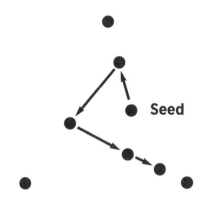

What would you expect?

It's rather like share price movements. They are limited in the direction and size of the move. And their next destination is linked to their previous one. So if share prices are random, unpredictable, as much anyway as the move of the Seed in the above example, then we would expect no pattern. In other words, forecasting would be impossible.

Instead, with the above game, the result is the following fractal – anything but random!

Figure 4.19: Fractal – anything but random

As traders we know what may be unpredictable at the level of second-by-second can nevertheless form a discernable, predictable pattern over time. Of course this does not mean we can forecast with mathematical precision, but it does mean there is more predictability than we may think.

In spread trading as with any type of trading we need to form some style of forecasting. I like to place more emphasis on trading, as forecasting sounds too long a task and we are mostly only concerned with short-term moves.

Spread trading allows you to do both – forecast and trade. You will create a portfolio that will include long-term investments that will be made up not only of stocks, but currencies, like GBPUSD or EURJPY or commodities like GOLD, BRENT, or CORN, with more and more markets being added each month.

As an example of the challenges in different time scales, take Google's share price intraday over five days in the chart below and compare it to a less random-looking pattern over a period of months.

Figure 4.20 - 5 days of Google

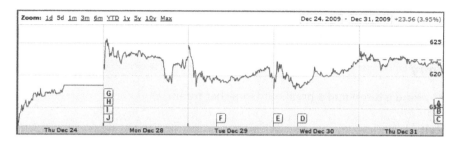

Source: Google

Figure 4.21 - 6 months of Google

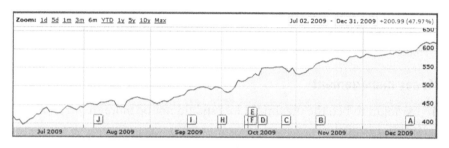

Source: Google

We must not mix time frames when we trade, as you can see they show two different stories of where the stock for Google may be heading

Now let's look at a couple of strategies.

Strategy 1: The Breakout

This is one of the simple trading strategies which works because it incorporates good trading practice and principles.

Entry

1. Find a trend and a breakout from that trend.

Exit

2. Set a profit level greater than a stop-loss level. The stop-loss should be the point beneath the trend line, where if the price returns we would know we were wrong in the trade. I.e. if a breakout is genuine, then the price should stay above the trend line in the direction of the breakout.

3. Even if markets are random, if your profit targets are greater than your loss targets, then you should be profitable.

Money management

4. Amount to bet: the maximum loss should not be more than 2% of your trading capital.

Variations

Take profit might be at a 'two-bar' low, etc.

Figure 4.22: Breakout

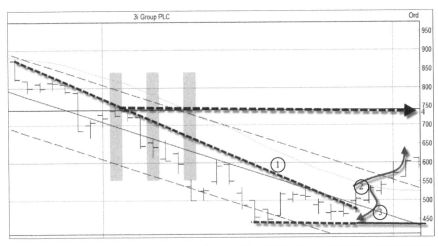

Created by Alpesh using Alpesh Patel Special Edition of Sharescope

Example: 3i Group

1. Find a trend, e.g. downward trend (1).

2. Locate a breakout from that trend to the upside (2) as a purchase point.

3. Set a stop-loss, i.e. know when you are wrong and price resumes downward trend (3).

4. Set a profit target based on a reasonable recent price level (4).

5. Ensure reward target (reward – entry) is greater than risk (i.e. entry – stop-loss), i.e. (4-2) > (2-3).

6. Trade size should be such that the amount you could lose is less than 2% of total portfolio value, i.e. 2% < (2-3).

Aggressive option: If price is halfway between entry and profit target, then double stake and move stop-loss to entry price.

Strategy 2: MACD (Mac-D)

Difficulty Level: Intermediate to Advanced.

The primary indicator is the MACD which can highlight divergences – that is, the price is making divergence. For bullish momentum, the MACD is making higher lows (its low bases are rising) and the price is not doing the same. The idea is the price too will start rising.

I use the MACD to confirm my view of a stock and I use the Stochastic and RSI to support the MACD. I have also found that when the Bollinger Bands (see lines on the following chart) are close together, this can indicate that a sharp price move is about to happen.

Bullish signals

Bullish Divergence: Here I am looking for the *MACD* to make a higher low and the price not to. (See the diagram where price makes a lower low). I look to enter when the price eventually starts moving higher too.

1. I want the *Stochastic* if possible to make a similar pattern (i.e. higher lows), but if it does not it is not necessarily a negative.

2. I want to see the *RSI* also make a series of higher lows, but it is not vital.

3. I tend to find if the *Bollinger Bands* (see the lines on the main chart) are close together then that can suggest a large price move is imminent.

4. I usually wait before buying for the price to move above the previous day's high, or a two day high if I am being more cautious.

5. I always check the company news to ensure there is nothing negative and, ideally, that recent comment from the company or about the company is positive.

6. I check my *Breadth radar* graph setting. Usually, I am not bullish if the '*New Highs-Lows*' is on a downward trend. Equally I am more short-term bullish if it is trending higher. I check the *Correlation* graph to ensure it is not too high (as a rough guide above 0.7 is high). Ideally, if I am going to beat the FTSE 100 or Dow, then there is little point picking stocks highly correlated to them.

When to sell and close the above position

1. The *MACD* starts flattening out, moves horizontally, and is in an overbought position.

2. The *Stochastic* and *RSI* usually, but not always, start moving lower or making 'bearish divergences'.

3. The price makes a 2 day low (1 day low if I am very risk averse).

4. I may close half my position and let half run if I am undecided.

Opposite is the Price, MACD, Stochastic and RSI.

Figure 4.23: Price, MACD, Stochastic and RSI

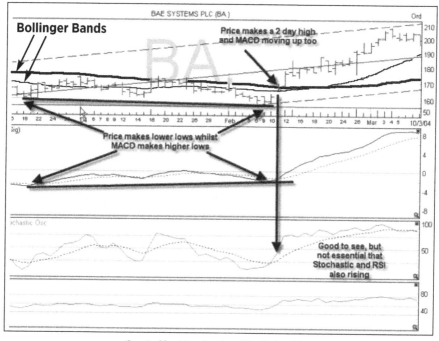

Created by Alpesh using Alpesh Patel Special Edition of Sharescope

Bearish signals

Bearish Divergence: Here I am looking for the *MACD* to make a lower high and the price to make a higher high. I look to enter when the price starts moving lower, perhaps a 2 day low, preferably on some overall bad market or company news.

1. I want the *Stochastic* if possible to make a similar pattern (i.e. lower highs), but if it does not it is not necessarily going to stop me making the trade.

2. I want to see the *RSI* also make a series of lower highs, but it is not vital.

3. I tend to find if the *Bollinger Bands* are close together then that can confirm with the above signals that a large price move is imminent.

When to buy and close the above position

1. The *MACD* starts flattening out, moves horizontally, and is in an oversold position.

2. The *Stochastic* and RSI usually, but not always, start moving higher or making bullish divergences.

3. The price makes a 2 day high (1 day high if I am very risk averse).

I may close half my position and let half run if I am undecided as to whether the trend may continue.

Figure 4.24: Where to buy and close

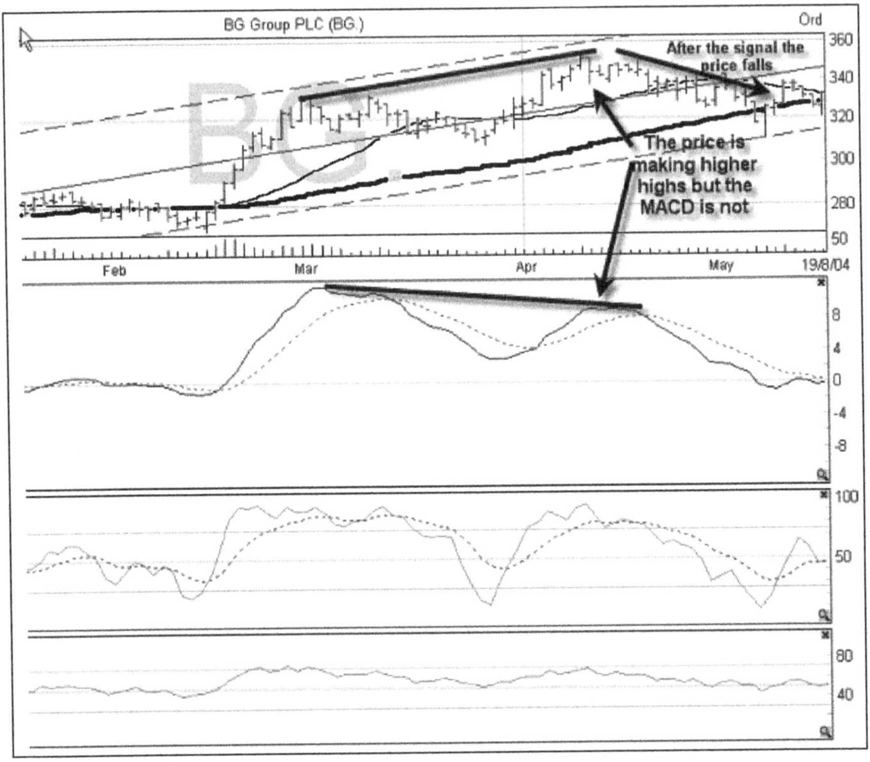

Created by Alpesh using Alpesh Patel Special Edition of Sharescope

Note: the indicators mentioned above are available on most spread trading platforms.

I don't intend to go through all the meanings as we only need to know how to apply the skills and how to read the indicators – but for those who are interested:

■ **MACD** (Moving Average Convergence Divergence) is an oscillator that is calculated by taking the difference between two exponential moving averages. A signal line is also plotted to help with interpretation. It is used to identify overbought and oversold conditions.

- The **Stochastic Oscillator** is another indicator often used to identify when the market is overbought or oversold.

- The **RSI** indicator measures a share's performance relative to its own recent price moves. It too can be used to gauge overbought and oversold conditions.

- **Bollinger Bands** are bands displayed on top of the share price. The width between the bands varies depending on the volatility of the share price. The greater the width the more volatile the share price, the narrower the width the less volatile the share price.

These indicators are shown in the following chart.

Figure 4.25: The indicators

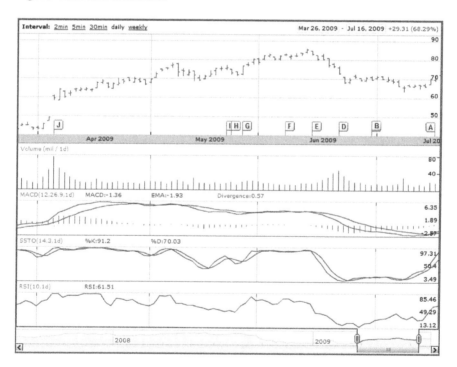

Created by Alpesh using Alpesh Patel Special Edition of Sharescope

Above is the chart for RIMM (Research in Motion), showing the price, then the MACD, then the Stochastic and finally RSI.

The MACD shows the bearish divergence around mid-June 2009 with the price starting to decline. The Stochastic tends to anticipate bearish nature a couple of days earlier and the RSI even before that.

The characteristics of winning strategies

Winners had strategies which not only worked but they appreciated that traders do not do things which are too difficult or are only effective at certain times. So their strategies had a common consistency across market conditions and reliability – they didn't just work sometimes.

Figure 4.26: characteristics of winning strategies

Reliable

Tested and proven

Easy to follow and remember once practiced

Work in all markets – bullish and bearish and sideways

Rewarding, profitable without being gambling & NOT with lots of losing trades for a few big winning ones.

Summary

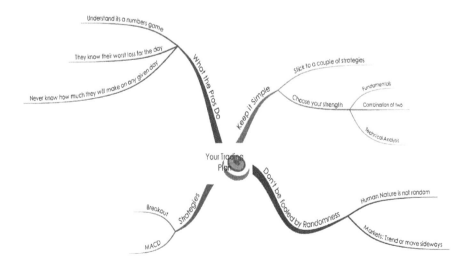

Created by Paresh Kiri

Chapter 5

How Winners Manage Risk

"Whatever you hold in your mind will tend to occur in your life. If you continue to believe as you have always believed, you will continue to act as you have always acted. If you continue to act as you have always acted, you will continue to get what you have always gotten. If you want different results in your life or your work, all you have to do is change your mind."

— **Anon**

So how much money do winners start with?

From one FX broker we found too small an account size and your chances of being profitable diminished – presumably because of costs (see the following Figure).

Figure 5.1: Analysis of account size and profitability

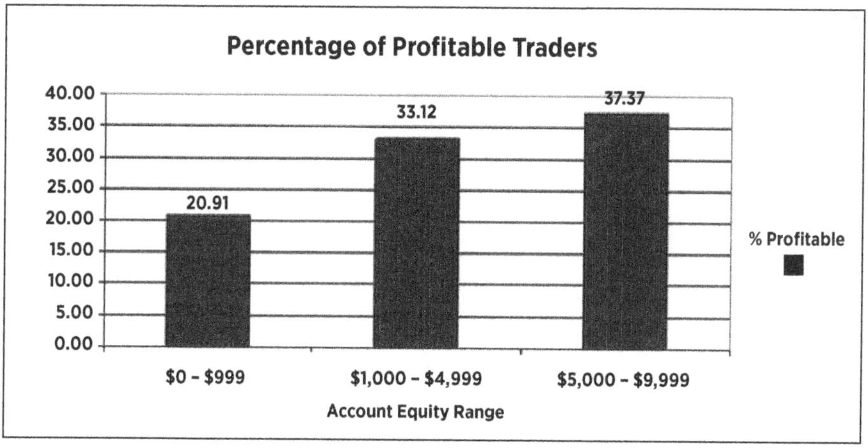

Percentage of Profitable Traders

Account Equity Range	% Profitable
$0 – $999	20.91
$1,000 – $4,999	33.12
$5,000 – $9,999	37.37

Source: FXCm

We found that once a trade had risen 10% into profit, if it fell back to break-even, you were less likely to make money on it if you held on, than if you exited. From the trades we analysed, winning traders did not let winning trades turn into losers.

Winners were quicker to exit at a loss is another way to put this. They were quicker and so took smaller losses. Losers were more likely to hold on and took bigger losses as a result.

We even found a spread bettor who was overall profitable, but was wrong more times than he was right. In other words he made more on his winning trades than his losing trades – even though he had more losing trades. This is another way of saying, he would take lots of small losses than risk them becoming big losses.

We found more winners traded forex than any other product. Now we cannot readily say that they were cleverer, more experienced or that forex is easier and more profitable. All we can say is that more winners traded forex.

The reasons the winners we interviewed gave for why they traded forex, and in some cases found forex easier, was that "it had smoother trends", "it reverts back to where it was" and "it moves in cycles". Albeit, some did note that since the Euro crisis the market has changed somewhat, being more volatile and harder to trade.

Figure 5.2 The 10 most popular spread betting instruments and their relative popularity

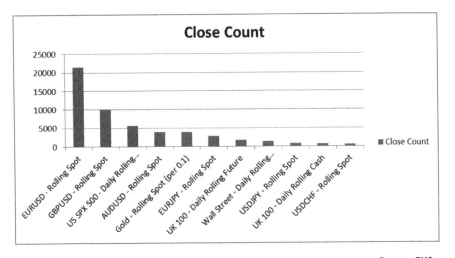

Source: FXCm

Tip: Those who bet small amounts but did more trades were more profitable than those trading big size but infrequently.

We found that winners did not make a few big trades. Winners bet smaller sums (measured as a proportion of the money in their account) than losers who tended to risk more money. Winners bet small sums often, which is how they made a decent return on their capital. Of course if they bet a few small bets, then despite being a winner, they would not be a good winner (making, say, 20% return on their account size).

Winners were ones who bet small and often. Losers either bet big and infrequently or bet big and often, thereby depleting their account. Some of the losers may well have gone on to be winners, had they not wiped out their accounts in their first ten trades. Looking at the range of trades they placed – other than that their trade size as a proportion of their account was large –

you could not tell if they were more accurate or less accurate at being right. In other words, a loser and winner may over ten trades both have been right five times out of ten. But the loser will have lost 80% and the winner broken even.

Your stake

> **If you know how much money to put into each trade you will make more money than those focused on just making profits.**

Spread trading is about making money of course. But to make money you need to know how much money to put into each trade. That will, as much as calling the market right or wrong, determine how much money you make and keep.

One such rule is that if you know the stock could drop by amount X before you exit, then that amount you could lose should be 2% of your total capital. I keep it that simple. In fact, all professionals keep it that simple! The reason is if I have a string of five losing trades, then I am down 10%. Not too bad. Most people after five losing trades are down 50%!

Look at the table below. If your portfolio loses 20%, then you need to achieve a 25% gain to break-even. 25% is more than even Warren Buffett's long-term average. The point is, make sure you do not even make a paltry 20% loss. It is easily lost.

Loss of capital (%)	Gain needed to recover (%)
5	5.3
10	11.1
15	17.6
20	25.0
25	33.3
30	42.9
35	53.8
40	66.7
45	81.8
50	100.0
55	122.0
60	150.0

So the point is look at the figures. It is why the world's best traders cut their losses short and quickly. Phone in to any TV programme and ask any stock-picking analyst who appears on TV, "If my portfolio drops 30% as a result of your stock-pick, how much does it need to rise to break-even?"

I guarantee they will not know.

Look at the figure below. Notice how the percent to recover increases exponentially as the loss increases.

Figure 5.3: Showing % recover against % loss

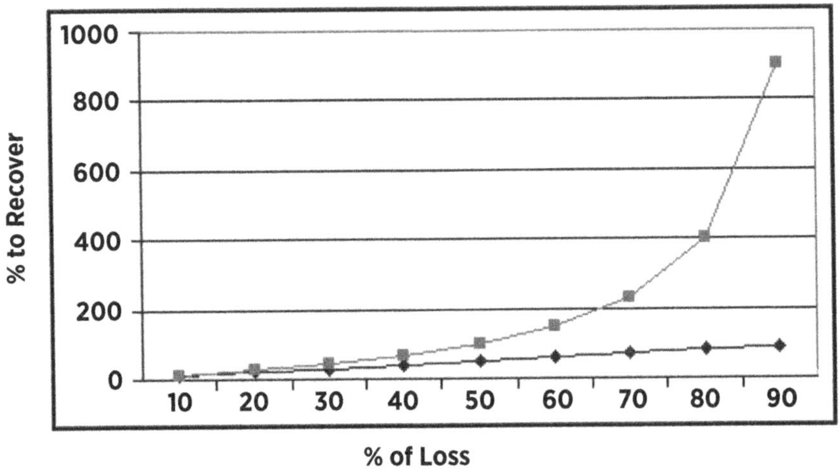

Proven by PhDs in a simple exercise

An experiment was conducted involving forty people with doctorate degrees. The doctorates were asked to trade on a computer. They started with $10,000 and were given 100 trials playing a game in which they would win 60% of the time. When they won, they won the amount of money they risked in that trial. When they lost, they lost the amount of money they risked in that trial.

How many PhDs made money at the end of the experiment?

Two!

The other 38 lost money. 95% of these very academically smart people lost money playing a game in which the odds of winning were better than any odds in Las Vegas.

Long trades took longer to make money than short trades

When we analysed closed profitable trades versus the number of days from open to close, we found that long trades took longer, on average about twice as long, to exit at a profit than short trades. More importantly, the reward measured by how much you earned per day of holding open a long trade versus a short trade was much less for long trades.

So, all other things being equal, you're more likely to earn money quicker when prices are falling than when they are rising.

"If it's good at $100, it ain't better at $80"

When we put the proposition to our sample group of winning and losing spread bettors "Is a stock that has fallen from $100 to $80, better value, all other things being equal?" and therefore the implication being you should buy more – the difference between winners and losers was that the winners saw a fall as a reason to sell, whereas losers saw it as a reason to buy.

Sooner or later you will ask yourself whether you should add to a losing stock position. The reasoning will be tempting: "If it was good at $100, then it must be better at $80." Such lore is especially popular on online bulletin boards.

But stop. This and other trading myths are costly, yet pervasive – they burrow around in online portals waiting for the unwitting. Read what the professional traders say first and it will save you money.

Take 'buying more at a lower price', other variations of this include, 'pyramiding'. The idea is that by buying more stock as the price falls, you reduce your average purchase price and so lower your break-even point.

For instance, if you bought $5,000 of Microsoft stock at $100, then another $5,000 worth when the stock halved in price to $50, the point at which you would break-even moves from $100 to only $66. It is tempting.

Don't do it.

Trading is not about getting a win on any one trade; it is about limiting your losses and maximising your gains over all your trades. If you average down then you're simply less diversified and own twice as much of a company whose price keeps falling. That's fine if you think it is the best place out of 3,000 listed stocks for your money, but bad if you just want to 'get a win'.

Moreover, novice investors often confuse price with value.

A falling price does not mean a cheaper stock. The value of a stock can be measured by earnings, the assets it holds, and other ways. A falling price could reflect simply lower expectations of value.

The investor should instead consider, "In which stock can I best make a return?" It would be a great coincidence if the answer is, "The very same one which has been returning me a loss".

If a stock drops 90%, you may well reason it does not have further to fall and is worth a punt or worth keeping hold of, or even buying more. Indeed, some investors only look for such stocks.

Well, if a stock is down 90%, you would probably concede that it could easily move down 95%. What is the change in value of your investment if that happens? No, not 5%, but 50%, because if a stock drops 90%, then halves, it is down 95%.

The problem is private investors often make investment decisions on where the price once was ($100), rather than where it is now ($10) which is why they reason, "Surely being down 90%, it does not have much further to go".

Would you normally be willing to accept a 50% loss?

Perversely we are more willing to accept a relatively large loss (50%) if we have already suffered even larger losses (90%).

The professional investor does not think like that. The correct reasoning should be, "Where can I get the best return for the risk I am willing to take at this point – in this investment or some other?"

Winners performance was skewed, as you'd expect, but in a manner you may find surprising

We found winners mimicked successful professional traders in their win/loss profiles. Of course, professional traders would be trading with much more money, but spread betting winners' returns distributions looked the same.

Opposite we show a professional forex trader's win/loss distribution of returns.

Figure 5.4: A trader's win/loss distribution of returns

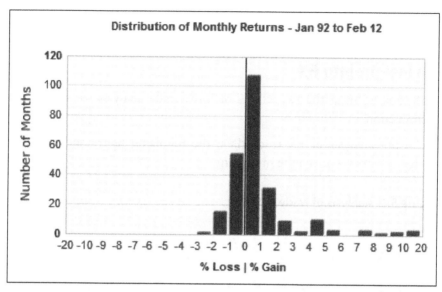

Source: Hathersage Asset Management

The winning spread bettors who had been trading the longest and been most successful mimicked these types of data spreads.

The point to note with winners was that they had a few big winning months, very few big losing months. And most of their trades won a little and lost a little.

Whereas losers had a few big losing months, very few big winning months and most of their trades also lost a little and won a little.

So what is the difference between winners and losers?

Winners had a way of ensuring very few big losing months. They also had a way of ensuring big winning months. Losers didn't.

How did winners do this?

For some, they added to winning positions. Others never let a winning trade become a losing trade once it was up 10% for instance. Others had tight stop-losses at which they exited. They would not wait on a loser. They would never add to losing trades. Some winners had the attitude that each trade at the start is a 50-50 gamble and so you bet small. Once you know it is moving in your direction, you add more money. If it is not, you exit quick. Losers did the opposite. They exited their winning trades to pay for their losing trades, to which they added even more money in an attempt to lower their average break-even point.

An insight into FX

Let's look again at the two charts of forex trade analysis we saw in the Introduction.

Following analysis of FX trade data, the following figure shows which currency pairs produced the most wins.

Figure 5.5: Analysis of trade data

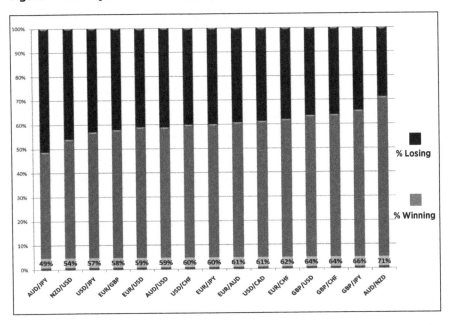

Source: FXCM

The following figure shows that overall, as we know, traders lose money. But the easiest pair in which to make money is AUD/JPY. It is not clear why it should be this one. The numbers are 'pips' or FX points.

Figure 5.6: AUD/JPY

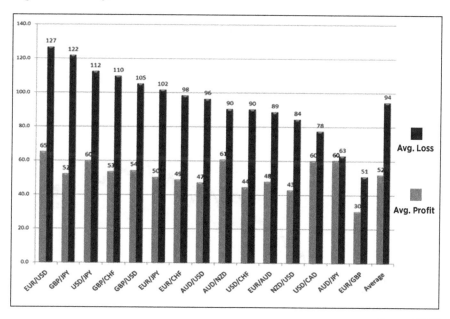

Source: FXCM

You may use the above insights to decide which currencies you would focus on when spread betting. We see that as a sensible way to approach the market. Every advantage counts after all.

Winners and losers had roughly the same number of winning-to-losing trades

In a way we have discussed this already. It was not that losers kept on having losing trades. It was that some of their losing trades wiped out their winning trades. After all, if they kept on losing, they would do the opposite of what they are doing. Instead, it was that winners and losers were close to 50-50 winning to losing trades (for those who were high frequency traders as opposed to the few buy and hold traders who hold for long periods).

Winners simply did not have, or had very few, big losing trades. Losers also held onto losing trades on average longer than winners held onto losing trades.

Do winners use stop-losses?

The following figure shows two lines and the hypothetical returns from a basic RSI trading strategy on USD/CHF using a 60 minute chart. This system was developed to mimic the strategy followed by a very large number of FX clients, who tend to be range traders. The lower line shows the raw returns, if we run the system without any stops or limits. The higher line shows the results if we use stops and limits. The improved results are plain to see.

Figure 5.7: Raw returns v. using stop-losses and limits

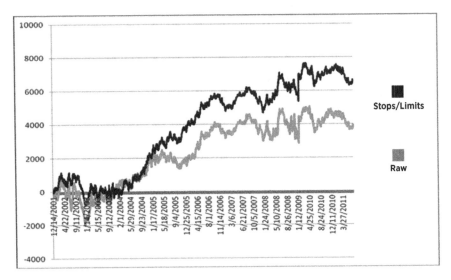

Source: FXCM

How do winners determine the downside risk on any one trade?

A risk/reward of 1:1 or higher was more profitable than one that was lower. The following chart shows a simulation for setting a stop to 110 pips on every trade. The system had the best overall profit at around the 1:1 and 1:1.5 risk/reward level. In the chart below, the left axis shows you the overall return generated over time by the system. The bottom axis shows the risk/reward ratios. You can see the steep rise right at the 1:1 level. At higher risk/reward levels, the results are broadly similar to the 1:1 level.

Again, we note that our model strategy in this case is a high probability range trading strategy, so a low risk/reward ratio is likely to work well. With a trending strategy, we would expect better results at a higher risk/reward, as trends can continue in your favour for far longer than a range-bound price move.

Figure 5.8: Simulation for setting a stop

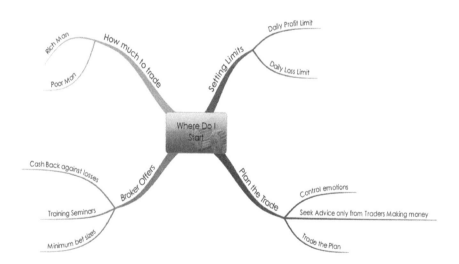

Source: FXCM

Summary

© Paresh Kiri

Appendix

A Primer on Charting

A quick overview of charts used by spread bettors

Figure A1: Open, High, Low, Close Price Bar

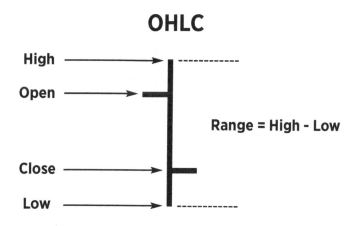

Figure A2: Trends

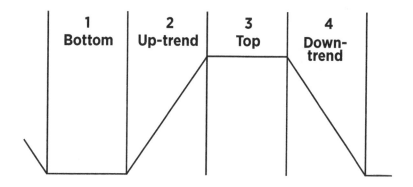

Figure A3: Candlestick charts

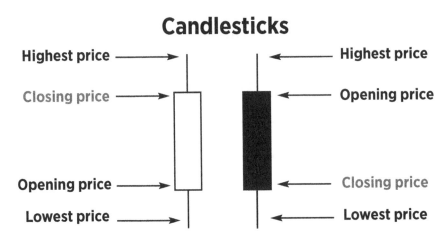

Candlesticks

The body is filled if the open is higher than the close

Figure A4: Patterns in Japanese candlesticks suggesting price reversal

Candlesticks Reversal Signals

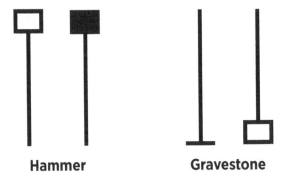

Hammer   Gravestone

Figure A5: Another Japanese candlestick reversal pattern

Dark Cloud Cover – Reversal

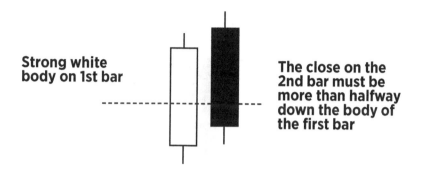

Strong white body on 1st bar

The close on the 2nd bar must be more than halfway down the body of the first bar

Reversal signal after an up-trend

Figure A6: Price reversal pattern

Morning Star – Reversal

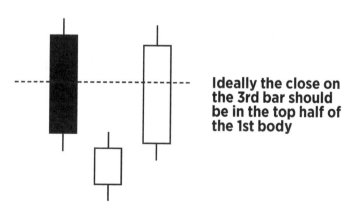

Ideally the close on the 3rd bar should be in the top half of the 1st body

Figure A7: Price reversal

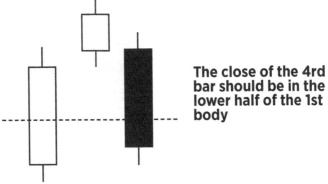

Evening Star – Reversal

The close of the 4rd bar should be in the lower half of the 1st body

Figure A8: Trend

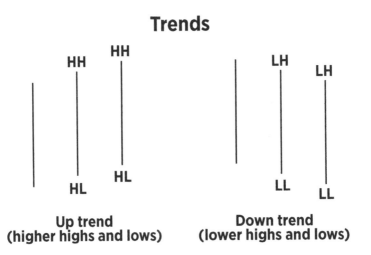

Trends

**Up trend
(higher highs and lows)**

**Down trend
(lower highs and lows)**

Figure A9: Trend start and end

Trends: Start and End

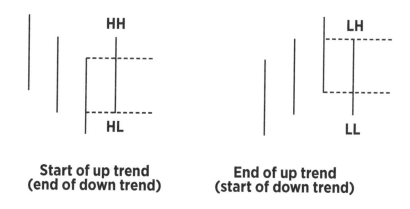

**Start of up trend
(end of down trend)**

**End of up trend
(start of down trend)**

Figure A10: A popular price chart pattern

Trends: Head and Shoulders

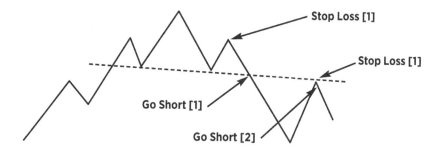

[1] Go short when price breaks below the neck line. Place stop-loss above the last peak. [2] If price rallies back to the neck line, go short on a reversal signal and place a stop-loss above the resistance level.

Figure A11: Inverted Head & Shoulders Pattern

Inverted Head and Shoulders

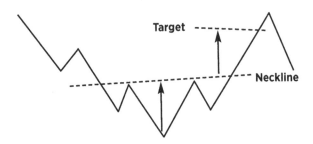

The target is measured vertically from the lowest trough to the neckline (drawn through the peaks on either side). It is then projected upwards from the breakout above the neckline.

Figure A12: When TV talking heads talk about 'Support'

Support Level

The support level is stronger every time that price respects the support line and/or if high volumes are traded at the support level.

Figure A13: Support & Resistance

Support becomes Resistance

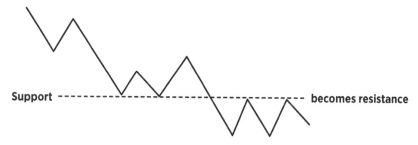

Support -------- becomes resistance

Once penetrated, the support level may act as a resistance level. Stockholders who bought at the support level will be inclined to sell when price rallies back to that level, to recover their losses.

Figure A14: What analysts mean by stop-loss

Stop-Loss

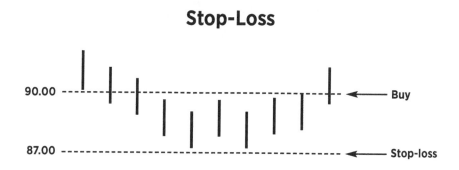

90.00 ◄──── Buy

87.00 ◄──── Stop-loss

Example of a stop-loss: Stock purchased at $90.00 and stop-loss placed at $87.00 (below the recent Low).

OFFER FOR ALL READERS

Register free at www.alpeshpatel.com and receive:

- My market views in your inbox.
- Research I personally use from exclusive sources such as Goldman Sachs.
- Free access to my seminars & online webinars.
- Free online trading education videos.

Index

R

Renaissance Technologies 21
research 35, 38
return on assets (ROA) 43
return on equity (ROE) 42-3
return on investment (ROI) 43
return on time 23
risk/reward ratio 100
RSI 83, 84, 85-6, 87

S

sales growth 38
Seykota, Ed xiv
short-term traders 7
shorting xiii, 7
Simons, James 21
Soros, George 17, 18, 21
Spreadex x
stochastics 12, 83, 84, 85-6, 87
stop-losses 99-100, 111
    levels 11, 82
support & resistance 76, 110-1

T

technical analysis 12, 76, 79, 105-111
technology 24
timing, *see trading*
trading
    amount per trade 93
    capital 8, 14, 23, 82, 91-4
    efficiency 35-6
    frequency 7-8, 92
    full time 21-2
    online v by phone 12-13
    signals 13
    systems 12
    timing 8, 12, 70-2
trendlines 12
trends 3, 108-9
Tropin, Kenneth xiv
Tudor Jones, Paul xiv

V

value 96
volatility 5

W

winners
    becoming losers 15
    methods & strategies 21, 23, 67,
        70, 88, 91, 92, 97
    mimicking 17, 96-7
    number of 15, 99
    trading efficiency 35-6

Lightning Source UK Ltd.
Milton Keynes UK
UKOW06f0652100616

275972UK00004B/131/P